"Just as race and economics ~~church~~, so can age. A generation gap has created a conundrum for the faith. Young folks are leaving the church, and old institutions are hemorrhaging. But this book is a sign of hope—a conversation bridging the generational gap. Here is a dialogue reminiscent of Paul and Timothy, a reminder that the old folks need youth and the young folks need elders. We must dream together about the future of the faith. The church must be both ancient and fresh, rich with tradition and winsome with imagination. There's that ancient prophecy from Joel, quoted again in the book of Acts, 'your young men will see visions and your old men will dream dreams.' On these pages a young man and an old man dream together. And they are joined by a stunning cast of faith leaders who chime in along the way. *The Future of Our Faith* is simultaneously an invitation to accept the church as it is and to dream of the church as it could be."

—**Shane Claiborne**, author and activist
(www.redletterchristians.org)

"I have long looked to Ron Sider for his wise counsel, and I increasingly look to Ben Lowe for his leadership on issues of faith and justice. At this critical time in the church's history, I am grateful for their new book, *The Future of Our Faith: An Intergenerational Conversation on Critical Issues Facing the Church*. This book is an invitation and a challenge for us to partner across generations for the sake of the kingdom."

—**Noel Castellanos**, CEO and president, Christian
Community Development Association (CCDA)

"The church needs more intergenerational conversations. It needs even more intergenerational conversations that are as rooted in scripture, as grounded in current-day struggles, and as fruitful as this honest and important dialogue between Ron

Sider and Ben Lowe is. *The Future of Our Faith* will be a blessing to the church today and a model for the church to come."

—**Karen Swallow Prior**, author of *Booked: Literature in the Soul of Me* and *Fierce Convictions—The Extraordinary Life of Hannah More: Poet, Reformer, Abolitionist*

"Gathered here is a wealth of wisdom, conviction, and hope from two leaders who refreshingly defy tired religious and political categories. If you care about the future of Christian witness in a post-Christian America, you'll read *The Future of Our Faith*."

—**Katelyn Beaty**, managing editor, *Christianity Today*

"There are generational divides on some of our most pressing issues, and there are sincere and faithful voices on both sides. The problem is that the generations often talk past each other rather than listen to each other. *The Future of Our Faith* is a multifaceted examination of the hazards and hopes of our time across generational lines. Ron Sider and Ben Lowe are two of the best Christian thinkers I know. I can't imagine a more dynamic duo to write a book like this."

—**Jonathan Merritt**, author of *Jesus Is Better Than You Imagined*

"While I don't agree with everything in this book, the conversation here is thought-provoking and a great help for Christians seeking to analyze the world around us. The discussion between Ron Sider and Ben Lowe ought to remind us of what we are often sadly lacking in the evangelical church—cross-generational connection. I pray this book sparks many more conversations between older and younger Christians about the future of our faith."

—**Russell Moore**, president, Southern Baptist Ethics and Religious Liberty Commission

THE
FUTURE
OF OUR
FAITH

An Intergenerational Conversation
on Critical Issues Facing the Church

RONALD J. SIDER AND BEN LOWE

BrazosPress
a division of Baker Publishing Group
www.BrazosPress.com

© 2016 by Ronald J. Sider and Ben Lowe

Published by Brazos Press
a division of Baker Publishing Group
P.O. Box 6287, Grand Rapids, MI 49516-6287
www.brazospress.com

Printed in the United States of America

Library of Congress Cataloging-in-Publication Data

Names: Sider, Ronald J.
Title: The future of our faith : an intergenerational conversation on critical issues facing the church / Ronald J. Sider and Ben Lowe.
Description: Grand Rapids, MI : Brazos Press, 2016. | Includes bibliographical references.
Identifiers: LCCN 2015037139 | ISBN 9781587433719 (pbk.)
Subjects: LCSH: Christianity—Forecasting. | Church. | Intergenerational relations—Religious aspects—Christianity.
Classification: LCC BR145.3 .S53 2016 | DDC 277.3/083—dc23 LC record available at http://lccn.loc.gov/2015037139

16   17   18   19   20   21   22   7   6   5   4   3   2   1

In keeping with biblical principles of creation stewardship, Baker Publishing Group advocates the responsible use of our natural resources. As a member of the Green Press Initiative, our company uses recycled paper when possible. The text paper of this book is composed in part of post-consumer waste.

To my six granddaughters
with the hope that they
experience life in its fullness.
—RS

● ● ●

To God
for reconciling us into the body of Christ.

And to my parents
for pointing me and so many others to God.
—BL

Contents

Part 2 Ben Lowe's Chapters (with Ron Sider's Responses)

Acknowledgments

From Ronald Sider
Many thanks to Ben Pitzen, my student assistant at Palmer Seminary at Eastern University, who did a superb job typing my manuscript for me and finding materials.

From Ben Lowe
With love and thanks to:

Mom, Dad, Gram, Uncle Art, Nat, Ellen, Jude, the Kampung Clan, and the rest of our family.

Eric Norregaard for writing the discussion questions and offering feedback on yet another one of my writing projects.

Josh Martin, for being my roommate through another book. And for being so patient and helpful about it.

My colleagues at the Evangelical Environmental Network, Young Evangelicals for Climate Action, and the Au Sable Institute—for your inspiration, encouragement, and prayers.

Diane Swierenga, the Norquist family, Rob Gallagher, Fred Hickernell, Noah Toly, Jamie Aten, Peter and Miranda Harris,

Fred and Linda Van Dyke, and Vince and Ellen Morris—for your counsel, support, and friendship.

Ryan Cherry, Nate Liu, Pascal Ramadhani, Jenn Carver, Ellen Leahy, Liz Dong, Cheryl Wenzlaff, Wil and Katie Maxey, Jerry Liu, Jonathan Kindberg, and other good friends—for being community.

Jason Fileta, Jenny Yang, Christena Cleveland, and Gabe Salguero—for kindly contributing the sidebars to my chapters.

The good folks at Baker Publishing Group and Brazos Press, particularly Bob Hosack—for taking on this book.

And, finally, Ron—for giving me an opportunity to write with someone I deeply respect and have learned so much from.

1

Why This Conversation

It doesn't take being part of the Christian faith for very long before tensions between older and younger generations become apparent. We don't see eye to eye on many things, whether it's about stylistic issues such as worship music or Sunday attire, or about doctrinal or ethical issues such as sexuality or social justice. Such tensions are to be expected as incumbent generations seek to safeguard the traditions and institutions they have painstakingly built up, while rising generations react against the status quo and push reforms. Such conflict can be particularly heightened in immigrant contexts, as the second generation strives to assimilate into the new surrounding culture while the parents' generation struggles to conserve their heritage.

As a result of these generational clashes, however, some younger Christians are finding church irrelevant and are leaving. Many of those who stay are increasingly frustrated and disillusioned by the track record of Christianity on a number of fronts. Older Christians still run most churches, denominations, and ministries today and are both upset and concerned by some things younger Christians say about many topics including sex, the Bible, social action, and church doctrine.

God has entrusted us with a remarkable mission—to be his children and representatives in a broken and hurting world. Generational clashes, while not the only fault line running through the church, detract from this good work and hamper our faithfulness. The world is changing and so is the church. Where are we headed? How can we all fit in together on this journey? How can we find better ways forward?

We Need to Talk

A few years ago, I (Ron) published an article in *Relevant* magazine expressing my appreciation for millennials while articulating four key questions I have for this rising generation. I heard that my article was widely read, but I wondered how my questions were being received. At the time the article was published, Ben was passing through Philadelphia (where I live), so I gave him a copy of the article and asked for his feedback.

I (Ben) read Ron's article with interest while on the plane back from Philadelphia to my home in Chicago. He ended the article by inviting a dialogue with my generation. So, a few days later, I wrote back with my own set of questions—questions for all of our generations to address together—about key problems in the church that his generation is handing down to us. A conversation started, and the idea for this book was born.

Our premise here is that there's a lot of talking and writing *about* each other's generation but much less talking and writing *with* each other. Intentional, charitable, and constructive dialogue is the way to build bridges between our generations and begin moving forward together. It's easier for each generation to be defensive of itself and critical of others. But the reality is that we all have strengths and weaknesses, and we all get some things right and others wrong. There's a lot we need to learn, and we can't afford to give up on one another.

Older generations are deeply concerned about retaining younger generations in church but have to decide how much to reach out, be open, and share leadership and control. Younger generations don't just need to be protected or contained—they also need to be empowered and commissioned.

Younger generations are known for reacting against the status quo; but instead of walking out in self-righteous anger or disaffection, they have to decide how much they're willing to humble themselves, value the good in their heritage, and find constructive ways to reform the bad. Raised in an often sheltered, neutered, and controlled faith, younger generations desire to be authentic and not shy away from hard questions and real struggles. They also need to respect those who have gone before them and realize that their generation too will make many mistakes.

What This Book Is and What It Isn't

First, this book is about discussing key issues facing the church today. It's not an exhaustive list of generational differences, however, and it's also not about debating preferences such as music styles or Bible translations. There's a place and time for those discussions, but they shouldn't be what defines us. Instead, we've each picked four areas that we believe will inform American Christianity in the twenty-first century. In the first part of the book, I (Ron) have contributed four chapters focused, respectively, on evangelism, relativism, marriage, and homosexuality. Each of my chapters is followed by a response from Ben. In the second part of the book, I (Ben) have contributed four chapters focused, respectively, on discipleship, politics, unity, and God's creation. Each of these chapters is followed by a response from Ron. We've written this introduction and the conclusion together. Each chapter also includes discussion questions contributed by Eric Norregaard, who is a good friend and writer/editor from the generation in between ours.

Second, this is a dialogue, not a debate. We're writing from distinct generational contexts and perspectives—we're almost half a century apart in age! While we may approach things differently, however, the point is not to disagree (we often don't) but to better understand each other so that we can find common ground and constructive ways to move forward together. Indeed, there's much that we agree on from each other's chapters, even if we don't specifically affirm or highlight each overlapping area in our responses. So anyone looking for heated debate will be disappointed.

Third, we're writing primarily to Christians who care about the future of the church and are confused or frustrated by the tensions and differences between generations. This includes younger Christians who can be critical of how incumbent leaders have been running things and who are determined to avoid making the same mistakes. It also includes older Christians who are concerned that rising generations are too ungrateful and reactionary and are rejecting many of the very values that they were raised on. At the same time, however, we hope this discussion remains accessible even to those who don't identify as followers of Jesus. There is, after all, a lot of interest in how American Christianity may or may not be changing as new generations transition into leadership.

Fourth, we're writing primarily from and to the American church. This is who we are and where we come from. The body of Christ is incredibly diverse—even just in the United States—and we make no claim to represent everyone. At the same time, we pray that much of this dialogue will still be meaningful to our sisters and brothers from all around the world.

Fifth, finally, while we can't claim to speak *for* our respective generations, we do speak *from* them. Both of us are deeply committed to the faith and have been heavily involved in the church for years (one of us for a few more years than the other!). And we both long to see a church united in Christ's love across all boundaries—including generational divisions—that faithfully proclaims and embodies the gospel of the kingdom of God.

Our Starting Point

The overarching message of this book is straightforward: there are growing intergenerational tensions in the family of God over what it means to be faithful today, and we need to find better ways to sort these things out.

But this takes working together across our generations, and it starts with each of us being willing to sit down and have a conversation. Every generation has its strengths and weaknesses, its prophetic visions and cultural blind spots. We won't always agree on everything, but that doesn't mean we can't learn and grow together. Instead of just complaining about each other, what could it look like for us to talk with each other more?

I (Ben) am grateful for the faith and leadership of those who have come before my generation. I'm also deeply grateful for the many elders who graciously seek our input and welcome our influence. We stand on the shoulders of our parents and grandparents, and they've done so much for us. At times we may react arrogantly against our heritage and the status quo or push too impatiently for change. I pray that through conversations such as this one, we will be able to better understand, value, and love each other, and that this will enable us all to hear God more clearly and move forward more faithfully together.

I (Ron) consider this kind of conversation a very high privilege. That young people fifty or more years younger than I am consider it worthwhile to listen to my views is a gift I highly treasure. In an important way I am amazed that young people who communicate via tweets and selfies using their smartphones still want to dialogue with me, who at their age experienced radio and black-and-white television as the hot new means of communication. I do not take for granted that ongoing interest in dialogue. I think that interest must be earned and nurtured as seniors like me seek to listen respectfully to today's young Christians as carefully as we hope they will listen to us. In many respects, my part of this book represents a heartfelt thank you to young people ready for that kind of intergenerational dialogue.

PART 1

Ron Sider's Chapters

(with Ben Lowe's Responses)

2

Will You Remember Evangelism?

RON SIDER

My first question is simple: Do you care as much about the fact that billions of people do not have a living relationship with Jesus Christ as you do about the social injustice that ravages the lives of billions of needy neighbors? Are you spending as much time, energy, and resources on evangelism as on social action?

Believe me, I am absolutely delighted that this generation of young evangelicals demonstrates a passion for social justice. I have devoted a great deal of my life to begging, urging, and pleading with evangelical Christians of my generation to become far more deeply engaged in combating poverty, economic injustice, racism, war, and environmental degradation. It thrills me to see how your generation of Christians demonstrates a rigorous engagement on these issues.

A few years ago, I spoke again at the chapel at Wheaton College. Just before I rose to speak, the president of the college leaned over and said, "This generation of Wheaton College students shares your concerns more deeply than any previous generation." Obviously I was pleased. That this generation of young evangelicals has a strong passion for social justice is simply splendid.

But I also feel a lurking uneasiness. I am a historian by training, and I remember that one hundred years ago a terrible split rent American Christianity. One wing of the church, called the Social Gospel movement, developed a passion for challenging a variety of social injustices in American society. And they did a great deal of good. Tragically, however, the Social Gospel folk often embraced a liberal theology that abandoned crucial parts of historic Christian theology. They also largely neglected evangelism. The result has been a catastrophic decline in "mainline historic Protestant" denominations like the Episcopalians, Presbyterians, United Methodists, and the United Church of Christ.

The response to this Social Gospel movement (by the Christians we now call evangelicals) was to focus almost exclusively on evangelism. They ignored the strong biblical call to empower the poor, correct social injustice, and work for peace. I remember one older, prominent evangelical leader telling me in 1975 as he joined in supporting the beginnings of Evangelicals for Social Action: "Ron, I have been going to evangelical Bible conferences for sixty years, and I never heard a sermon on what the Bible says about social justice."

That huge split between the Social Gospel movement and evangelicals marred many decades of the twentieth century. Both sides were unbiblically one-sided.

Fortunately, in the last forty years, there has been major change, especially in the evangelical world. Forty years ago, most evangelical leaders agreed that "saving souls is the primary mission of the church." Slowly, more and more evangelicals embraced the view that biblical faith calls us to do both evangelism and social action. By the Third World Congress sponsored by the Lausanne Committee for World Evangelization in Capetown, South Africa, in 2010, virtually everyone agreed with this both/and understanding. And this generation of young evangelicals, thank God, simply assumes this holistic approach.

So why am I uneasy? In my lifetime, I watched as some young evangelicals (back when I could still count myself as one of them!) became so frustrated with the failure of older evangelicals to work against racism and economic injustice that they slowly lost their commitment to biblical authority, historic orthodoxy, and evangelism. And even some of those who maintained their commitment to biblical revelation devoted most of their energy to social action and failed to do evangelism. Sometimes they rightly condemned heavy-handed, insensitive evangelistic tactics—but then failed to develop better evangelistic methods. The wrongheaded evangelistic strategies of some evangelicals became an excuse for not doing evangelism at all. Besides, they felt, they were fully preoccupied with social action to make the world more just.

As I look at young evangelicals today, I worry that something similar may be happening. Thank God for the new, widely adopted conferences on justice. Thank God for all the new movements and organizations where young evangelicals are working for peace, justice, and creation care. But do you still grieve over the fact that a couple billion neighbors have never heard of Christ as much as you do that more than a billion people struggle to survive on $1.25 a day? What a tragedy if this generation of Christians repeats the mistakes of the old Social Gospel movement and provokes a new evangelical/Social Gospel split like the one that devastated the church in the last century.

A truly biblical understanding of many basic Christian teachings demands that we embrace both evangelism and social action. I note these: the nature of persons; the character of sin; the gospel; and the person, teaching, and uniqueness of Christ.

The Nature of Persons

Long ago, the great Greek philosopher Plato said that persons have a good soul trapped in an evil body and that our spiritual side is what is truly important. Over the centuries this Platonic one-sidedness has misled Christians to neglect the material side of humanity. (The modern evangelical focus on "saving souls"—rather than whole persons—is just one illustration.) But the Bible teaches that persons are "body-soul" unities. The body is so good that the Creator of the universe became flesh in the incarnation. The body is so good that Jesus rose bodily from the dead—and promises to give us resurrected *bodies* when he returns. That Jesus devoted a great deal of potential preaching time to healing sick bodies simply underlines how biblical faith corrects Plato's one-sided understanding.

But the biblical view is equally critical of the modern (and ancient) materialistic view that persons are merely complex machines. At death, we do not just die and rot as the great naturalistic philosopher Bertrand Russell said. At death, believers graduate to life eternal in the presence of the Risen Lord. Jesus said it is better to lose the whole world (everything in our material space-time world) than lose one's relationship with the living God (Mark 8:36).

If persons are "body-soul" unities, then the only way to solve all our problems is by combining evangelism and social action. The story of my good friend James Dennis underlines this point. Brother James and I were both elders in an inner-city, interracial congregation in the 1980s. One day he told me that if he had met me twenty-five years earlier when he was an angry black militant, he might have killed me. I'm glad he met Jesus first! But before that happened, his life fell apart. He was abusing alcohol and his marriage was disintegrating. In fact, a major crime landed him in prison. But in prison, he met Jesus Christ. And when he left prison, Christ helped put his life back together. His marriage and family were restored, he found a good job, and our church offered important support.

If anyone thinks that all Brother James needed was improvements in his socioeconomic, material situation (i.e., job training and better housing), they don't have a clue. Brother James needed a living relationship with Jesus Christ. That transformed his whole being, values, and character. At the same time, if anyone thinks all he needed was to be "born again" without any changes in racist educational systems for his children and racist practices in employment and housing, they don't have a clue either!

Brother James needed both inner spiritual transformation and more just socioeconomic structures. He needed evangelism to lead him to Christ and social action to correct unjust structures—precisely because he and each of us are not just a "body," not just a "soul," but a body-soul unity. Any either/or strategy to transform his life would have been inadequate. That is why holistic, evangelical community development programs like those modeled and advocated by people like John Perkins work better. They produce more lasting, more complete transformation than programs that work at only one-half of the problem.

The Character of Sin

The biblical teaching on sin leads to the same conclusion. In more recent decades, evangelical preachers have largely defined sin in personal terms—lying, stealing, and committing adultery. Liberal preachers focused on social sin—unjust, racist social structures. The funny thing about the Bible is that God seems to care about both. The prophet Amos condemns Israel because "they trample on the heads of the poor / as on the dust of the ground / and deny justice to the oppressed. / Father and son use the same girl /and so profane my holy name" (Amos 2:7). God will send the nation into captivity both because of their economic oppression of the poor and because of their sexual misconduct![1]

I think younger evangelicals understand the reality of social sin or structural injustice better than older evangelicals.[2] You understand that racist or economically unjust social systems are huge barriers to human well-being and that they must be corrected.

But here too we must avoid one-sided thinking. A great deal of modern thought since the Enlightenment suggests that the evil in the world is simply the result of bad structures and cultures that twist and distort human beings who are born good. All we need to do to correct the evil in the world, we are told, is construct better educational, social, and economic systems. (Karl Marx said that if we just abolished private property, which is the cause, he said, of the economic injustice in the world, we would create new, essentially good human beings.)

The biblical understanding of sin is much more profound. The human problem is far deeper than unjust structures— although they certainly need correcting. Because of the fall, every person is profoundly selfish. It is the accumulation of self-centered actions by individuals that become embedded in culture, legislation, and socioeconomic structures that create structural injustice. So if the ultimate cause of evil social systems is the self-centeredness at the core of each individual, then no amount of structural change *by itself* can solve the human problem. We need evangelism to change individual persons and social action to correct unfair systems.

The Gospel

Many, many evangelicals of my generation and earlier have preached an individualistic, one-sided gospel that is flatly heretical. They reduced the gospel to the forgiveness of one's sins made possible by Christ's substitutionary atonement on the cross so that we could go to heaven when we die. That is not Jesus's gospel!

Jesus said the gospel is the good news of the kingdom (Mark 1:14–15).[3] Jesus meant that the messianic time, promised by the prophets, was actually breaking into the present in his person and work. In their prophecy about the future messianic time, the prophets had promised that there would be a new, vertical, right relationship with God and new horizontal relationships of justice and peace with neighbors. Jesus taught both. He certainly offered God's unconditional forgiveness to sinners and died on the cross to atone for our sin. But he also preached and brought new concrete, material socioeconomic transformation as he healed the sick; cared for the poor; treated lepers and women as dignified persons, equal to others; and called his followers to love their enemies. Jesus's circle of disciples was a new community, a new social order, already beginning to live out the reality of Jesus's dawning messianic kingdom. You certainly cannot preach Jesus's gospel of the kingdom and only do evangelism.

But some people so emphasize the socioeconomic aspects of Jesus's kingdom that they neglect the forgiveness of sins. They reduce the gospel to correcting economic injustice and working for peace among nations. That is also unbiblical and heretical.

Jesus said the long-expected messianic kingdom was actually breaking into the present. But he was equally clear that that kingdom had not arrived in its fullness. Sin, injustice, and even death itself continued to rampage through society. The fullness of the kingdom would come only at Christ's return. Only then would all brokenness, structural injustice, and evil disappear.

The fact that Jesus's messianic kingdom has begun but is not yet complete means that persons can come into a living relationship with Jesus Christ and be on their way to living eternally with the Lord even though they still are trapped in evil, unjust social structures. Jesus promised the thief on the cross that "today" he would be with him in paradise, even though Jesus did not change his current, dreadful real-life situation (Luke 23:43). Black slaves came to a living relationship with Christ even while their "Christian" slave masters treated them brutally. Desperately poor people around the world come to know Christ and are on the way to life eternal even as they slowly die of malnutrition. Obviously, it is terribly wrong for Christians to seek to evangelize oppressed, malnourished persons without trying to end their oppression and correct the systems that devastate their lives. But it is nonetheless true and important to see that very oppressed, very poor, even starving people can hear the gospel, embrace Christ, and be on the way to life eternal even while their human condition is unjust and exceedingly displeasing to God. We should never wait to share the gospel until we have corrected societal evils, just as we dare never evangelize persons without seeking to end their structural oppression.

Jesus's gospel—unlike so many one-sided Christian understandings of the gospel—includes two crucial aspects. Central to Jesus's gospel is that God longs to forgive prodigal sons and daughters and has accomplished that forgiveness at the cross. Equally central to Jesus's gospel is the fact that a new, messianic socioeconomic order has broken into history with Jesus and his disciples. It is now being modeled (imperfectly, alas) in the church but will be completed at Christ's second coming. The only way to share Jesus's whole gospel is to combine evangelism and work for justice and peace.

It is very important to see that evangelism and social action are inseparably interrelated—even though they are not identical. Evangelism is that set of activities whose primary intention is inviting non-Christians to embrace the gospel of the kingdom, believe in Jesus Christ as personal Lord and Savior, and join his redeemed community. Social action is that set of activities whose primary goal is improving the physical, socioeconomic, and political well-being of people in this life through relief, development, and structural change.[4]

The inseparable relationship between evangelism and social action is crucial.[5] Evangelism promotes social action because, as we saw in the case of my friend James Dennis, born-again persons live differently and thereby transform society one person and one family at a time. Also important is the fact that the common life of the church (when the church indeed lives like Jesus) profoundly shapes and improves the whole society. It was churches who cared about the poor and needy, who first started schools for poor children and hospitals for the sick. Later, society as a whole embraced what Christians had begun. Social action even has an evangelistic dimension. How? When Christians demonstrate their love in the name of Christ to poor, needy persons, the result is much greater openness to the gospel. And finally, social action protects the fruit of evangelism. William Booth, the founder of the Salvation Army, used to say that unjust social systems encourage vice and atheism, whereas just systems make it easier to live the way Christ taught. If there were many more good-paying jobs in our inner cities, it would be much easier for inner-city youth to resist the temptation to make easy money by selling drugs. In all kinds of ways, evangelism and social action are very closely interrelated. In actual practice, it is often impossible to say where the one ends and the other begins. We share the gospel both with our words and our deeds.

But there is another crucial misunderstanding to avoid. Evangelism and social action are not identical.[6] In my lifetime, many Christians (especially ecumenical Christians and liberation theologians) said their social action was evangelism. Then they proceeded to devote all their time to working against racism and economic injustice. They almost never devoted any effort or time to telling people about Jesus Christ or inviting them to accept Christ. But they said they were doing evangelism—because social action, they said, *is* evangelism.

We can do important social action without talking about Jesus. But we cannot do evangelism without words—words about who Jesus is. In fact, if Christians do social action without saying that Jesus is the reason they do it, their social action simply makes them look good. It merely points to their caring behavior rather than pointing to Christ.

Several things show that evangelism and social action are not identical. First, they have different intentions and outcomes. Successful social action aims at and leads to cleaner water, better health, less starvation, more democracy, and greater social justice. But by itself it does not lead to a living relationship with Jesus Christ. While in South Africa in 1979, I met a wonderful Jewish activist fighting to end apartheid. As we talked for hours, he gave me a great political education. But one evening, I had the opportunity to invite him to accept Christ and he did. I could have worked for a decade with this Jewish friend, fighting apartheid—and that would have been a good thing to do. But that would not have been identical with inviting him to Christ. The outcome of the social action might have been helping to end a racist system. The outcome of the evangelistic invitation was a person on the way to life eternal. God desires both outcomes, but they are far from identical.

Second, equating evangelism and social action endangers the practice of evangelism. If everything that Christians are sent into the world to do is evangelism, then the special task of inviting non-Christians to embrace the Savior easily gets lost. And that is precisely what has happened in many circles.

Third, it is confusing to talk about evangelizing social structures. Unjust social structures desperately need to be changed. But multinational corporations and Chinese or American legal and political institutions cannot accept Jesus as personal Lord and Savior, experience baptism (even if you only sprinkle!), join a local church, take communion, experience daily fellowship with the Holy Spirit, and look forward to personal bodily resurrection at Christ's return. Only persons can do that. We can correct and improve socioeconomic structures—and thereby make them better reflect biblical norms.[7] But we cannot evangelize them. Evangelism and social action are distinct, even though they are closely, inseparably, interrelated.

I have a friend who was a student at Moody Bible Institute in the late 1960s. He felt called to the city and just assumed that evangelism would be important in his work. But he wanted to let his actions speak for him. So he moved into the inner city and for a decade worked starting some excellent programs (a medical clinic, etc.), improving the lives of very needy people. But when, at the end of ten years, he reflected carefully on his ministry, he realized that he had not actually invited people to accept Christ. He had helped persons experience better health and improved socioeconomic well-being, but these persons had not been transformed by the power of the gospel, and their lives had not changed significantly.[8]

That is an easy trap to fall into. It would be easy for this generation of young evangelicals to be so preoccupied with social injustice and so annoyed with inappropriate evangelistic techniques of an older generation that they fail to invite people to accept Christ. If you make that mistake, people will, at best, only experience half of the change they need.

The Person, Teaching, and Uniqueness of Christ

Two other central biblical truths underline the importance of evangelism: Jesus is the only way to salvation; and people are lost without Christ.

My generation of evangelicals too often said these things arrogantly and harshly. Too often Christians have spoken of Christ as the only way, even as they participated as imperialistic colonizers in conquering and oppressing other nations and cultures. That has no integrity. We dare speak of Christ as the only way with integrity only as we are servants sacrificially ministering to the physical needs of non-Christians and struggling to end their oppression. Too often, also, Christians talked of being lost without Christ in a way that seemed to forget God's love. Any truly Christian discussion of being lost without Christ must begin and end with God's astonishing, overflowing love for everyone. But past mistakes dare not lead today's Christians to ignore clear biblical truths.

Again and again, the New Testament teaches that Jesus is the only way to salvation. "No one knows the Father except the Son and those to whom the Son chooses to reveal him" (Matt. 11:27). "I am the way, and the truth and the life," Jesus announces. "No one comes to the Father except through me" (John 14:6; see also 3:36). Just weeks after Jesus's crucifixion and resurrection, Peter declared to a Jerusalem crowd: "There is salvation in no one else, for there is no other name under heaven given among mortals by which we must be saved" (Acts 4:12 NRSV). "There is one God; there is also one mediator between God and humankind, Christ Jesus" (1 Tim. 2:5–6 NRSV; see also 1 Cor. 8:5–6).

Sometimes, contemporary Christians find it hard to affirm this biblical teaching that has been confessed by the church for two thousand years. How can we presume to say Jesus is the only way to salvation in a pluralistic world full of devout Muslims, Buddhists, Hindus, Sikhs, and so forth? Is not such a claim arrogant and disrespectful? Maybe Christians in earlier generations who knew only other Christians could say that, but is it not different with today's Christians who know more about other religions and frequently know their adherents as good personal friends? One-third of all people living today may claim to be Christians. But the other two-thirds believe in other ways to salvation. How can this Christian minority be so disrespectful of that large majority?

I think it is very important to remember who it was who first made this sweeping claim that Jesus was the only way to salvation. This astonishing claim was first made by a tiny, tiny group of Jesus's followers living in a powerful pagan empire full of a vast diversity of religious beliefs. These early Christians were an almost infinitesimally small fraction of all the people living at the time. Yet they presumed to declare boldly that Jesus was the only way to salvation. And they said so because they knew that Jesus the carpenter was God become flesh.

Jo Anne Lyon

General Superintendent, The Wesleyan Church

Evangelism is not an industry. However, it has taken on all the tenets of what we tend to think of as an industry: profit margins, bottom line, publishing, buildings, personalities, competition, institutions, and so on. Therefore, the purpose and effect get lost in all the complexities surrounding the pure form of evangelism.

Simply put, evangelism is inviting a person to come to Christ. When he or she becomes a Christ-follower, this becomes the beginning of a transforming process that starts in that person through the power of the Holy Spirit. It is in this journey that the Christ-follower begins to see the world through the eyes of Jesus and his desire to see restoration.

It is impossible to view the world through the eyes of Jesus and not see the inequities, the creation being destroyed, and the lack of value for life in all areas. For followers of Jesus, there is the mystic power of the Holy Spirit to bring about restorative justice. Frankly, this cannot happen in its fullness through any other entity except that of the community of believers.

It is in this context that evangelism and justice go together. They cannot be separated. Throughout Scripture they are intertwined as well. Historically, John Wesley and the revivals of England are excellent examples of evangelism and justice combined. The prophet Amos so aptly states it: "Let justice roll on like a river, righteousness like a never-failing stream!" (Amos 5:24).

But that declaration about the deity of the Nazarene carpenter makes their confession even more astonishing. Why? Because Jews were the least likely people in the first century to worship a carpenter and declare that he was God become flesh. There were lots of Greek and Roman polytheists in the first century who believed in many gods who sometimes became flesh. But Jews knew better. They were rigid monotheists. Their central belief was that there is only one God.

The amazing thing about the early Christians (originally *all* Jews) was that after the resurrection, they started saying things about the Nazarene carpenter that were clearly blasphemy—unless of course he was truly God in the flesh. After doubting Thomas met the risen Jesus, he uttered the words: "My Lord and my God" (John 20:28). Saul, the brilliant, highly trained Jewish monotheist, was so outraged at what the earliest Christians said and believed about Jesus that he led in their persecution and stoning. But after he met the Risen Jesus on the road to Damascus, he began to worship the carpenter.

For a monotheistic Jew, Paul's statement in Philippians 2:6–11 is utterly astounding. Christ Jesus, he wrote, was "in very nature God" but humbled himself, became flesh, and died on the cross. But the Risen Jesus is now exalted to "the highest place": "that at the name of Jesus every knee should bow, in heaven and on earth and under the earth, and every tongue acknowledge that Jesus Christ is Lord" (vv. 10–11).

In verses 10–11, Paul is clearly alluding to and partially quoting Isaiah, where Yahweh, the one God, mocks the idols and declares that they are nothing (Isa. 45:14–22). Yahweh declares that "before me every knee will bow; by me every tongue will swear" (45:23). Paul, the strictly trained Jewish monotheist, takes these words from the mouth of Yahweh and applies them to Jesus the carpenter from Nazareth. Jesus is God.

In fact, the word "Lord" used by Paul here and elsewhere to describe Jesus is the Greek word *kyrios*, used to translate the Hebrew word for Yahweh (the name of the one God) when Jewish scholars translated the Hebrew Bible into Greek in the second century BC. Beginning with the earliest letters (1 and 2 Thessalonians), Paul regularly begins his epistles with the phrase "God the Father and the Lord Jesus Christ."[9] At the center of early Christian faith embraced by devout Jewish monotheists was the astounding claim that a man from Nazareth should be prayed to and worshiped as God.

Something utterly earthshaking must have happened to persuade strict Jewish monotheists to do such a thing. Their simple explanation was that three days after his crucifixion (which for Jews totally demolished the credibility of anyone who claimed to be the long-expected Messiah), Jesus rose from the dead. The resurrection convinced these Jewish monotheists that Jesus was not only the Messiah but also Lord, God become flesh.

But if that is who Jesus truly is, if he is God Incarnate, then it is hardly surprising that he is the only way to salvation. Unlike pagan polytheists, Jewish monotheists knew that there are not lots of gods who can and do often take on human form. If the one God truly became flesh once, then we must submit to what he taught and tell everybody about it. If Jesus was only one of many great teachers, then of course it would be preposterous to claim that his way is the only way to salvation. But if the one God, the Creator of the universe, actually became flesh once, then it is not surprising that faith in God Incarnate is the only way to salvation for everyone. And just as clearly, it is the case that nothing is more important than telling everyone in the world about this fantastic news. When we know who Jesus truly is, evangelism becomes a joyful, urgent obligation.

But there is one other part of what the New Testament teaches that is particularly troubling to many contemporary Christians. Again and again, the New Testament says people are lost without Christ. Paul says that before they accepted Christ, the educated, religious Ephesians were "separate from Christ . . . without hope and without God in the world" (Eph. 2:12). Only when the Thessalonians accepted Christ were they rescued from coming wrath (1 Thess. 1:9–10). Again and again, Paul taught that the wages of sin is death—eternal death. Everyone has sinned and stands condemned under God's condemnation (Rom. 1–3). There is a coming day of judgment for all.[10] Those who do not embrace Christ will depart from the presence of the Living God (Rev. 20:11–15).

I understand why we hesitate to talk about this New Testament teaching about eternal separation from God. But it is precisely Jesus (the ultimate expression of God's overwhelming love for sinners) who says the most about this dread topic.

Jesus's parable of the sheep and the goats clearly teaches that everyone will appear before him at the final judgment. The righteous will enjoy eternal life in the presence of God. The wicked can only wait fearfully for the terrible words, "Depart from me, you who are cursed, into the eternal fire prepared for the devil and his angels" (Matt. 25:41). When Jesus explains the parable of the wheat and the weeds, he again speaks of final judgment. The Son of Man (Jesus's preferred title for himself) will throw all who cause sin and do evil "into the blazing furnace, where there will be weeping and gnashing of teeth" (Matt. 13:41–42; see also 13:49–50).

It is not entirely clear what Jesus means in Mark 3:28–29 by the unforgivable sin. But whatever it is, it clearly involves eternal separation from God. So terrible is the reality of eternal absence from the living God that Jesus recommends chopping off a hand or foot rather than living in sinful disobedience. "It is better for you to enter life maimed or crippled than to have two hands or two feet and be thrown into eternal fire" (Matt. 18:8).

Jesus's teaching on eternal separation from God raises very hard questions. What about those who have never heard about Christ? What about those who have refused to embrace Christ because of the sinful, wicked activity of people who called themselves Christians?[11]

I do not have complete answers to these questions. But three things are clear. First, the New Testament clearly teaches that God "desires everyone to be saved" (1 Tim. 2:4 NRSV), "not wanting anyone to perish" (2 Pet. 3:9). Second, God only holds people accountable for what they know, not what they do not know (Acts 17:29–30; Rom. 2:12–15; 5:13; John 15:22–24). And third, we can rest assured that our amazing God, who is the perfect combination of justice and mercy, holiness and love, will treat every person fairly. Because Jesus, who died for our sins on the cross, was raised on the third day, we know that God's final word is love and forgiveness.

Perhaps C. S. Lewis is right. God takes our freedom so seriously that God will allow us to choose to say no to him forever. Our loving God does not want that. He pleads with us to return and accept his love and forgiveness. But God will allow us, if we so choose, to depart eternally from his love.

Young Christians today must decide what to do with Jesus's teaching on eternal separation from God. If Jesus is just a great prophet, then of course we can ignore this part of his teaching as a tragic mistake. But if we believe with the early Christians and the church through the centuries that the carpenter from Nazareth is God in the flesh, then we must accept what he said. We dare not pick and choose among his teachings, selecting what feels good to us and our contemporaries and rejecting the rest. One fundamental test of the faithfulness of Christians today is whether they will dare to talk as much about the reality of eternal separation from the Living God as Jesus did.

By all means, we will not major on this topic. We will start and end with God's overflowing love in Jesus. But sometimes, we will dare to say that without Christ, people are lost—eternally. And knowing that will underline the urgency of evangelism.

A great deal of biblical teaching underlines the importance of evangelism: the nature of persons as body-soul unities; the fact that sin is personal and social; Jesus's gospel of the kingdom; and the person, teaching, and uniqueness of Jesus. My young friends, I beg you: please do not neglect evangelism as you rightly embrace the call to social justice.

Response by Ben Lowe

Concern is growing about whether my generation is committed enough to evangelism. I hear this a lot when working and speaking in churches and on campuses across the country.

Typically, it comes from Christian elders who have made evangelism—but not social action—a defining priority throughout their lives. What I find deeply compelling about Ron Sider is that he has done both. For decades now he has focused on engaging Christians in social action. My generation's passion here is at least partly the fruit of his ministry. Being a lifelong social justice leader gives Ron both the credibility and understanding to effectively engage us on our commitment to evangelism.

This is important because the topic of evangelism is loaded with baggage. As Ron acknowledged, Christians have a very mixed track record when it comes to using awkward, aggressive, or manipulative methods to "win people to Christ." We also haven't always been respectful or charitable in our views of and interactions with those who don't share our faith.

For better or worse, the broader society continues to change, and Christianity, while far from being marginalized overall, is not quite the dominant (or perhaps domineering) cultural force it once was. Billy Graham–style "crusades" that used to fill entire stadiums are fading into the past as America enters a more pluralistic, and even post-Christian, era.

Nonetheless, Christianity in America has been intertwined with our politics and culture for so long that in many circles it has become generic and watered down. According to the Pew Research Center's Religion and Public Life Project, 70 percent of Americans identify as Christian.[12] But how many of these 70 percent are active followers of Christ rather than cultural Christians by upbringing or socialization? In a country so superficially familiar with the gospel, being a Christian doesn't always mean much, and therefore evangelism faces a whole new set of challenges.

So for these and other reasons already discussed, many worry that my generation is swinging the historical pendulum away from evangelism and over to social action. There's at least some validity to this concern. I can easily think of friends and peers who have grown to embrace charity and justice but increasingly shy away from evangelism.

At the same time, however, I also know many others who care deeply about social action *and* are strongly committed to evangelism. I actually have more close friends involved full-time in specifically evangelistic missions than in social activism and advocacy. Some of these friends are serving with campus ministries across America, while others are teaching English in Asia or training church leaders across Africa. In each case they're finding that evangelism and social action really do go hand in hand; that pursuing God's mission in their contexts also includes addressing pollution, caring for orphans, working toward racial reconciliation, addressing political corruption, and more. If we're concerned about millennial Christians neglecting evangelism, the answer isn't to stifle enthusiasm for social action. Instead, we lift up examples such as these that powerfully showcase what holistic and integral mission looks like and why it matters.

This commitment to gospel proclamation isn't just anecdotal. At the end of 2013, the Barna Group released a study showing that millennials are actually growing in our commitment to evangelism. We're even surpassing the other generations here:

> While the evangelistic practices of all other generations have either declined or remained static in the past few years, Millennials are the only generation among whom evangelism is significantly on the rise. Their faith-sharing practices have escalated from 56% in 2010 to 65% in 2013. Not only that, but born again Millennials

share their faith more than any other generation today. Nearly two-thirds (65%) have presented the Gospel to another within the past year, in contrast to the national average of about half (52%) of born again Christians.[13]

It seems that the stereotype about my generation might not always be accurate. Regardless, of course, there's still a lot of room for growth in my generation and beyond when it comes to sharing our faith.

Here are five points on how I hope my generation—and the whole church—increasingly approaches evangelism.

First, our motivation for evangelism should be the same as our motivation for addressing social and environmental problems: love. Too often, we feel pushed into sharing our faith out of a sense of guilt. Or we view it as a challenge or competition to rack up as many converts as possible, akin to accumulating trophies on a shelf. This only ends up objectifying people as conversion targets, which is wrong. Besides, while we're called to share our faith, it's the Holy Spirit's role to convict and convert. If we truly love God and love our neighbor, as the Old Testament prioritizes and Jesus affirms, then we will naturally care about our neighbor's spiritual *and* physical well-being as well as their eternal *and* current well-being. We will want them to know Jesus Christ and his good news in all aspects and on all levels of life. Love must be why we engage in both evangelism and social action, and when others recognize and choose to receive our love, it's ultimately what will give us the right to be heard.

Second, social action is not just a door through which we can then "sneak in" the gospel. It's an integral part of God's gospel and mission as well. I've never had more opportunities to talk about my faith than while caring for creation or opposing injustice. Some might think this means we should use charity and justice work as merely tools to help us share the gospel.

Or perhaps we talk about it this way to justify ourselves before audiences that support evangelism and are suspicious of social action. This lacks integrity, however, and runs the risk of being manipulative and deceptive. It also devalues the work we're doing, which is good in and of itself. Missionaries serving in restricted countries may have to engage in a nonreligious trade or profession in order to gain entry, but that work then becomes a valuable part of their witness and worship. It's never just a tactic.

Third, we need to experience the saving and transforming power of Christ in our own lives in order to share it effectively with others. I wonder if sometimes the reason evangelism feels forced or unnatural is that we've grown distant from God and are not following in obedience. Authenticity is important and, in this consumerist age filled with many competing claims, people will expect to see that Jesus truly is changing our lives if they are to believe that he can change theirs too.

Fourth, too many evangelistic efforts have faltered due to poor follow-up. This is one reason why sharing our faith within the context of an ongoing friendship is particularly helpful and meaningful. In the Great Commission (Matt. 28:18–20), Jesus doesn't instruct his followers to go and make converts. He calls them to go and make disciples. We've typically not done a good job at this in the American church. Great emphasis is placed on bringing people to Christ, but we must invest much more effort in integrating people into our local churches where they can grow and serve as part of a community of faith. Being a Christian is not just about believing in God—even demons believe that and shudder (see James 2:19)—it's about becoming a lifelong follower of God.

Fifth, and finally, not everyone is called or gifted as an evangelist, but we're all called to share our faith. Similarly, not everyone is called to be a full-time activist, but we're all called to stand up for what is right and just. There are many callings in God's kingdom, and we all work together to make up the body of Christ. There isn't some magical formula for how much all of us must engage in activism versus evangelism, as if they truly can be separated from each other. Rather, we always seek to live justly and share our faith lovingly no matter where God leads and what God gives us to do.

DISCUSSION QUESTIONS

1. A core idea of this book is that leaders from different generations need to talk with each other. To what extent is your church leadership composed of people from different generations talking together and leading together? How do you feel about this?

2. For a scriptural look at the seamlessness of social justice and evangelism, take a look at Acts 4:32–35. Try to analyze which parts of the passage are talking about social justice and which parts about evangelism. What do you notice?

3. Outside of books and the media, where do you see social injustice with your own eyes in your daily life? Similarly, where do you see lost people with your own eyes in your daily life? If you compare your responses to these two questions, how do you think that affects your own view of the necessity of evangelism and/or social action?

4. If the Barna survey is correct—that the social justice–oriented generation of millennials is more involved in evangelism than previous generations of evangelicals—how

would you like to see your own church respond to that development?

5. Is there some way you can influence your church to move toward a more biblical understanding of Jesus's gospel of the kingdom and the inseparability of evangelism and social justice?

3

Will You Reaffirm Truth as You Learn from Postmodernism?

RON SIDER

Younger evangelicals have rightly learned from postmodernist thinkers that every person's ideas and beliefs are significantly shaped by one's specific historical location in space, time, and culture. And you have been appalled by the theological arrogance of too many previous evangelical thinkers and by the atrocious errors of even the best Christian theologians of earlier centuries.

Too often in the last century, evangelical thinkers have battled "theological liberalism" with a ferocity and certainty that seemed to suggest that they thought their own theological formulations were statements of absolute truth. They failed to see any strength or validity in other formulations and views. And they overstated the "biblical fidelity" of their own claims.

Furthermore, as one looks over the history of Christian thought, one sees that even the best theologians made horrendous mistakes. St. Augustine is perhaps the most influential theologian in Christian history. He penned numerous profound, biblically grounded books. But he also said dreadful things about sexuality and urged the state to kill heretics. Martin Luther wrote wonderful books about justification by faith alone, but he also claimed the pope was the antichrist and wrote terribly anti-Semitic things about the Jews. In my lifetime, too many older evangelicals were blatantly racist and homophobic. Many largely ignored the hundreds of biblical texts about God's amazing concern for justice for all, especially the poor and marginalized. A prominent older evangelical leader and former coeditor of *Christianity Today* confided to me about forty years ago that he had been going to evangelical Bible conferences for sixty years and never once heard a sermon on justice. How could the "defenders of biblical orthodoxy" be so unbiblical?

Younger evangelicals have rightly learned from postmodernism to be far more skeptical about any claim to truth. You reject an earlier philosophical foundationalism (stated dramatically by Descartes) that claimed to arrive at universally valid truth by reason alone. Descartes started with what he thought was a foundation of indisputable first principles and then sought to build an intellectual system that was absolute, objective, universally accessible, and valid. You appropriately agree with the majority of contemporary philosophers who reject foundationalism.[1]

You have also learned from postmodernist thinkers like Michel Foucault and Jacques Derrida that it is simply impossible to have a purely objective, fully accurate interpretation of any text—and that includes the Bible! Unless we are God, a double relativity affects us. Our interpretation of any text is shaped by and therefore relative to the presuppositions we bring. And all human presuppositions are relative.

Every person is a limited, finite individual deeply immersed in a particular culture that is different, often profoundly different, from the cultures described in an ancient text like Plato's or the Bible. Every reader brings a vast range of presuppositions from his or her own particular historical setting that prevents full, objective understanding of a text from the past.

Some postmodernist writers have overstated this point. For example, Roland Barthes, who emphasizes the independence of the reader from the author of a text, says, "The birth of the reader must be at the cost of the death of the author."[2]

In 1996, Dr. Alan Sokal, a physics professor at New York University, published an article in *Social Text* (a postmodernist journal) arguing that physical reality is merely a social and linguistic construct. He said that the idea of an external world that existed independently of any human mind was an out-of-date dogma of Enlightenment modernism. Physics, specifically quantum physics, is just a set of ideas constructed by subjective minds, not an accurate statement about reality discovered by a valid scientific method. The editors of *Social Text* thought the article (by a respected scientist!) supported their postmodernist ideas and published it.[3]

But Sokal promptly published a piece saying his article in *Social Text* was a hoax to call attention to the extremes of some postmodernist thought. And he invited anyone who thought the laws of physics were just subjective social conventions to jump out the window of his twenty-first-floor apartment.[4]

Christopher A. Hall

President of Renovaré

Postmodernism has it right and also quite wrong. Its vision is both clear and blurred. How so?

First, postmodernism helps Christians to recognize that all perceptions of "reality" come to us through the lens of the context in which we live, including our social, economic, racial, sexual, and church environments. Our understanding of our whole world, and of a host of ethical issues, is surely shaped—and sometimes no doubt distorted—by the community in which we are exercising our "reason." None of God's image-bearers is an autonomous, contextless mind. Postmodernism has helped us to see this.

Of even more immediate relevance to the church, postmodernism has reminded us that we are all deeply informed by our *Christian* environment too. Scripture possesses primary authority for Christians, but throughout history the Bible's interpretation has rightly been a communal endeavor, one guided and empowered by the Holy Spirit. We are instructed and shaped by each other; we need each other. This is what it is to be drawn by the Spirit into the "body of Christ." You might say that the Holy Spirit himself has a history, one that ripples through time in the thoughts and lives of all of God's image-bearers: Orthodox, Roman Catholic, Reformed, Anglican, Baptist, Lutheran, Independent Bible, and so on. We can never be independent of other believers, and we shouldn't try to be. Again, postmodernism has helped us to see this.

So where does postmodernism get it wrong? Whenever postmodernism affirms that "reality" is merely a social construction of the communal self, whenever it tells us that any and every version of reality (or that different and conflicting realities) can be right, since "rightness" depends solely on the creative community, it is dead wrong. Christians affirm that reality is, first and foremost, a creation of the living God, and therefore that it exists independent of me and my community. Reality is not invented by us, yet it can be known by us. Its truthfulness does not depend on our knowledge of it, though it is available to us to be known and even shaped, under God's hand.

> Above all, God has made himself known through Christ, a
> wonder revealed to us and not dependent upon our "yea" or
> "nay." Where postmodernism forgets this, it goes badly astray.
> The gospel invites us as a community to the triune glory at the
> center of reality and to be embraced by it. We enter into the glory
> as we listen to the authoritative voice of the Holy Spirit in the
> church's interpretive traditions and especially in the text of Holy
> Scripture, a text that addresses us, that can be understood by
> us, and that can lead us into the heart of reality itself.

The fact, however, that some postmodernist thinkers lapse into dangerous subjectivism does not invalidate their insistence that a totally objective interpretation of any text is impossible.[5]

Every single interpreter of the Bible—whether it be Luther, Calvin, a seminary professor, or you or I—is able at the very best to grasp a somewhat imperfect, always partial, and inevitably partly distorted understanding of what the biblical text says. There are two theological reasons for that: our finitude and our sinfulness. As finite human beings, we can see and know only a very limited amount. Furthermore, the fact that until death we are only partly sanctified means that our continuing sinfulness prompts us to interpret the Bible in ways that promote our bias and self-interest. Only God has a full, perfect understanding of the Bible. In this life, we Christians—even the best—can only see through a glass darkly (1 Cor. 13:12).

Younger evangelicals today rightly question, or at least insist on the right to rethink, the biblical interpretations and theological claims of my generation of Christians. You are certainly right in learning from postmodernism to question claims to truth.

But sometimes I wonder if you are abandoning truth altogether and embracing sweeping relativism.

Widespread Relativism in Contemporary Culture

I will never forget an incident in the Midwest more than a decade ago. I was speaking before an evangelical congregation pastored by a brilliant young evangelical leader who had recently obtained his PhD in philosophy from the University of Notre Dame. He told me that for the last seven years he had taught a catechetical class on the basics of Christian faith for younger teenagers in his congregation. Every year during the last session, he would set a glass container full of marbles in front of the class and ask: "How many marbles are in the glass?" As the students guessed the specific number, he wrote their answers on the blackboard. When everyone had suggested a number, he told the class that he had actually counted the marbles and there were exactly 135. Then he asked the class: "Which of your answers is closest to the truth?" Usually they agreed that it was the estimate closest to 135.

Next, he asked the class: "What is your favorite popular song?" As each person named a favorite, he wrote the title of that song on the blackboard. When the class finished with their song titles, he asked the question, "Now which of your songs is true or best?" Naturally, they always protested, saying that you cannot ask that question. Each person's preferred song is right for her. It is silly, perhaps intolerant, to say one preference is better than another.

Then, my friend told me, he would ask the question: "Is the statement 'Jesus rose from the tomb on the third day and he is true God as well as true man' more like the statement about the number of marbles or more like each person's personal feeling

about the songs?" And every year for seven years, this evangelical pastor told me, every single young person in the catechetical
class in this evangelical congregation said the statements about
Jesus were like one's personal feeling about the songs. Crucial,
central theological statements in Christian faith are not truth
statements. They are expressions of personal feeling relative to
each person's personal preferences.

I think that story points to a widespread relativism in contemporary culture. Many contemporaries think that each person rightly "constructs" her own religious beliefs and ethical
norms. Whatever I believe is right for me, and whatever you
believe is right for you. And no one should be so judgmental or intolerant as to suggest that someone else's beliefs are
wrong. Furthermore, one owes it to oneself to follow one's
inner feelings no matter how the resulting action may contradict historical understandings of morality. Human freedom
means that each person should construct his or her own religion
and morality. Not everyone, certainly not all Christians, goes
to this extreme. But this kind of relativism is widespread in
contemporary culture and has seeped deeply into the psyche
of many Christians.

Personal Freedom and Truth

Pope John Paul II wrote a brilliant encyclical, *The Splendor of
Truth* (*Veritatis Splendor*), which helps us understand this problem and its solution. Much modern thought, he argues, detaches
human freedom from truth. Each person, it is claimed, rightly
uses her personal freedom to create her own truth and morality.
"The individual conscience is accorded the status of a supreme
tribunal of moral judgment. . . . One's moral judgment is true
merely by the fact that it has its origin in the conscience. . . .

Such an outlook is quite congenial to an individualistic ethic wherein each individual is faced with his own truth."[6]

In response, John Paul develops what I believe is a biblical understanding of the relationship between truth and freedom. Genuine freedom depends on truth. "If you hold to my teaching [Jesus says], you are really my disciples. Then you will know the truth, and the truth will set you free" (John 8:31–32). It is a fundamental mistake for finite (and fallen) human beings to seek to create their own truth. God alone has the right to say what is right; and when we embrace that truth, we become truly free.

Modern relativism mistakenly thinks we achieve genuine freedom when we define our own "truth" and "morality." Biblical faith, on the other hand, urges us not to conform to this world but rather to be transformed by submitting to God's revelation of truth (Rom. 12:1–2).[7]

> Each day the Church looks to Christ with unfailing love, fully aware that the true and final answer to the problem of morality lies in him alone. In a particular way, it is *in the Crucified Christ that the Church finds the answer* to the question troubling so many people today: how can obedience to universal and unchanging moral norms respect the uniqueness and individuality of the person and not represent a threat to his freedom and dignity? . . . *The Crucified Christ reveals the authentic meaning of freedom; he lives it fully in the total gift of himself* and calls his disciples to share in his freedom. . . . Jesus, then, is the living personal summation of perfect freedom in total obedience to the will of God. His crucified flesh fully reveals the unbreakable bond between freedom and truth.[8]

Only as we turn to God's revelation of truth and morality can we escape modern relativism.

And it is essential that we do that. Finally, if truth and morality are simply subjective human constructs that individuals or different interest groups formulate to promote their self-interest, society collapses. If, as Nietzsche claimed, no moral truth exists, then society is simply a vicious power struggle where the most powerful trample the rest. As the famous atheist philosopher Bertrand Russell said, those who have the best poison gas will have the ethics of the future. That way leads to modern totalitarianism.[9] If we are to build good societies that respect the human rights of everyone, then we need to know that those rights and the definition of good come finally not from some human decision but from God.

Understanding Biblical Truth

To say that, of course, is not to claim that my definition of truth and morality is exactly what God reveals. Christian faith teaches that God has revealed truth and goodness partly in creation and far more clearly in the Bible. And what God has revealed is true. But we dare not confuse that claim with the far different assertion that my present understanding of biblical revelation is a full articulation of God's truth. As we have seen, every interpreter of the Bible is both finite and sinful. Our finitude means that we have only a very partial grasp of what God intends to tell us in the Bible. And our sinfulness means that we twist even what we partially understand to advance our own self-interest. Humility about all our theological and ethical affirmations is crucial—even though we are doing our best to listen with open minds to the Scriptures. If the greatest Christian thinkers like St. Augustine and Martin Luther got it very wrong at important points, we can be even more sure that we are making equally serious mistakes.

But that does not mean that truth does not exist. God knows all truth. Christ is the truth (John 14:6). All that the Bible intends to teach is God's revealed truth, even though my understanding of it is very inadequate. That God is Father, Son, and Holy Spirit; that Jesus is true God and true man; that Jesus rose bodily from the dead; that Jesus's life, death, and resurrection are the only way to salvation for everyone—these are unchanging truths that will always be essential for every generation of Christians, even though we finite human beings never fully understand them. Not everything must change.

Some people seem to think that the Bible can be made to say anything. And in fact, it is possible to cite somebody for almost any interpretation of a given biblical text—even the most absurd. But that certainly does not mean that one interpretation of a biblical text is as good or true as another. Even as we acknowledge that finite, sinful persons can never have a fully objective, fully accurate understanding of biblical revelation, we must seek to get closer and closer to biblical truth.

There are ways to avoid making the Bible a wax nose that can be twisted to say anything. Two things in particular help us avoid that: careful grammatical-historical exegesis and ongoing dialogue with the interpretation of the biblical text on the part of the whole body of Christ (both throughout history and across the world today).

To properly understand a biblical text (e.g., the book of Isaiah), we need a thorough understanding of the Hebrew language. We also need as much knowledge as possible about the history, sociology, politics, and so on of that time—including knowledge from archaeology. That means we need the help of scholars. Because we (and the scholars too) bring our modern presuppositions to the study of the text, we will never arrive at a fully accurate reading of the text. But more and more study of more and more detailed information about the Hebrew language and the history of that time will help us get closer to an accurate understanding of what the text actually says.[10]

But arriving at a fairly accurate understanding of what the text actually says is only part of our task of interpretation. The New Testament sets aside many things commanded in the Old Testament (e.g., circumcision, temple sacrifice, Deuteronomy's easy divorce laws). We need a canonical hermeneutic centered in Jesus Christ to understand what New Testament Christians should embrace.[11]

Even then, the task of learning what God wants to say to us today in the Bible is not over. For centuries, Christians thought that some biblical texts that reflected the view that the sun moved around the earth meant to reveal that this is precisely how the sun and earth relate to each other. Even Martin Luther denounced Copernicus for saying that the earth moves around the sun. And in fact, Psalm 96:10 says, "The world is firmly established, it cannot be moved." But we know from modern science that not only the earth moves around the sun, but the entire solar system (and galaxy!) is moving. Modern science helps us see that in Psalm 96:10 God was not trying to reveal to us something about the way the solar system works.

Nicholas Wolterstorff

Noah Porter Professor Emeritus of Philosophical Theology, Yale University; Senior Research Fellow, Institute for Advanced Studies in Culture, University of Virginia

Disagreement runs broad and deep among human beings, especially on moral and religious matters. It happens rather often that when college students gain some inkling of just how broad and deep is the river of disagreement on such matters, they give up on saying that those with whom they disagree are mistaken. They start thinking and saying that morality and religion are matters of preference, not of truth. Or they relativize truth to believers: "If I believe it, then it's true for me; if you believe the opposite, then that's true for you." Or they continue to believe that truth is nonrelative but go on to add that it's just too difficult to find out who's right and who's wrong. "Who's to say?"

There are serious philosophical problems with each of these positions. But on this occasion, let that pass. It has been my experience that almost always those who think and talk in one or another of these ways are living comfortable, privileged lives, and that a reality check is in order. If you were a Jew in Hitler's Germany, would you be tempted by any of these views? Would you be tempted to say that it's all a matter of preference? "Hitler prefers that I and my fellow Jews be murdered; we prefer that we not be murdered." Would you be tempted to say, "It's true for Hitler that it's a good thing to murder Jews, but it not true for those of us who are Jews"? Or imagine that you were being tortured: would you be tempted by any of these views?

We should all have the mental clarity and the moral courage to say that what Hitler did was profoundly evil, and that torture is wrong. Yes, in some cases it's hard to know what's right and what's wrong. But the cases are not all gray.

Grammatical-Historical Study

Properly understanding the truth God reveals to us in the Scriptures requires careful grammatical-historical study, a canonical hermeneutic centered on the Word become flesh, and also careful listening to contemporary knowledge.[12]

Listening to the vast number of biblical interpreters in church history and today provides a second safeguard against twisting the Bible to say what we want it to say rather than what it actually says. There is, of course, no one universal interpretation of any biblical text. Over the centuries, Christian exegetes and theologians have interpreted the Bible in many different ways. That is what we should expect to happen, since they were all finite, sinful persons shaped by the language and presuppositions of their particular setting. But on many central points of theology and morality there is considerable agreement. If our particular interpretation of biblical truth differs radically from that of the mainstream of Christian thought of the past and present, this should raise a huge warning sign. We should stop, probe deeply into why other Christians arrived at a different conclusion, and openly and carefully reexamine our own interpretation.

Careful grammatical-historical exegesis and extensive listening to the rest of the body of Christ will help us get closer to God's truth revealed in the Scriptures. But it is painfully obvious that it will not guarantee complete agreement in the global body of Christ. Roman Catholics, Orthodox, and Protestant Christians all believe that the Bible is God's special, reliable, truthful revelation. But in spite of centuries of study and a variety of efforts to listen to one another (far less than there should have been, to be sure!), we still cannot agree on some basic issues. Some Christians believe that the just war tradition articulates the most faithful understanding of what Jesus and the Bible reveal on the topic. Pacifists disagree. The same kind of fundamental disagreement persists about free will and predestination (e.g., Arminians and Calvinists), and the understanding of the Eucharist (physical presence of Christ vs. spiritual presence). In spite of centuries of honest searching and debate, devout Christians still embrace fundamentally different (and contradictory) positions.

Many Denominations

That is why, sadly, we need different denominations. If Christians were not finite and sinful, we would all embrace God's truth on these issues and could all be in one visible, united church. But in spite of centuries of effort, we have not been able to arrive at agreement. That does not mean that both sides of these historic divisions are equally right. I do not think that God thinks that pacifist and just war Christians or Arminian and Calvinist Christians are both equally right. Since they affirm contradictory views, at least one party in each debate must be wrong! But since Christians seem unable to reach common understanding on these and some other very substantial issues, we must sadly (because of our persisting finitude and sin) have different denominations that—at some important points—affirm contradictory positions about what they understand to be God's truth.

That does not mean we dare rest comfortably in our different denominational silos. We should exercise much more vigorous, persistent efforts to listen together to the Scriptures and revisit our historical disagreements on the things that divide us. Equally important, we must organize and strengthen ecumenical tables where we affirm and celebrate what we have in common. In spite of continuing disagreement on a number of significant issues, Roman Catholics, Orthodox Christians, and Protestants (at least those who still believe the historic creeds of those different traditions) all confess together that God is Father, Son, and Holy Spirit; Jesus is true God and true man and the only way to salvation for everyone; Jesus died for our sins on the cross and rose bodily from the dead on the third day; the Bible is God's fully reliable special revelation; and Christ will return some day to complete his victory over sin, evil, and death. That is a lot of common ground! We should focus more on our agreement than our disagreements even as we persist in major efforts to overcome those disagreements.[13]

The fact that Christians have not been able to resolve important differences on significant theological issues, however, does not mean that truth does not exist. It does not mean that God (who knows all truth) has no view on these issues. God knows the truth about the debate between Arminians and Calvinists and pacifists and just war folk. Truth exists. We are just too sinful, too finite, too trapped by our particular sociohistorical presuppositions to be able to gain a full understanding of truth. But we should keep searching—via more careful biblical study and more listening to the whole church. As we do so, we will inch closer to God's truth.

Tolerance versus Relativism

One final point. Please don't fall into the widespread contemporary confusion between tolerance and relativism. In so many circles, it is considered intolerant to say that someone else's beliefs and behavior are wrong. Whatever I feel is right is right for me, and it is disrespectful and intolerant for someone else to say I am wrong. That is a dreadful misunderstanding of what genuine intolerance is.

Tolerance in society means that I will respect the rights of other citizens to state views that I consider intellectually false and morally wrong. In fact, it means I will work vigorously to defend their right to say such things. It even means that I will love them, respect them as persons created in the image of God, and listen carefully to their arguments.

But that by no means implies that if I want to be tolerant, I must abandon the claim that such a person is wrong. Precisely when I argue that another person or view is false or wrong (even dangerously wrong), I am being tolerant as long as I am respectful and truthful in my disagreement and rejection of another person's views. Tolerance combined with vigorous, honest debate about our disagreements is precisely what is needed in a society where different people hold radically divergent, fundamentally contradictory views. Relativism obscures those differences. In fact, it makes a genuine search for truth impossible.

Jesus's command "Do not judge, or you too will be judged" (Matt. 7:1) has been grossly misunderstood both in the larger society and the church. The view is widespread that this statement of Jesus means that we should not criticize anyone else's theological views or behavior. We should abandon the practice of church discipline. We should think only about the log in our own eye, not the speck in the other's eye (Matt. 7:2–5). What Jesus says, however, is that we should *first* take care of the log in our own eye "and then you will see clearly to take the speck out of your neighbor's eye" (v. 5 NRSV).

If Jesus meant to say that we should never judge others, then he flatly contradicted his own teaching. Jesus harshly condemned the Pharisees as snakes and hypocrites (Matt. 23:15–36). He called Herod a fox (Luke 13:32). And Jesus specifically ordered us to exercise church discipline in the body of Christ—even to the point of excluding unrepentant people from the church (Matt. 18:15–17). And 1 John denounced the person who denied basic Christological truths about who Jesus was and is as a liar and the antichrist (1 John 2:22–23; 4:2–3).

Galatians 6:1–2 shows us how to judge others in the body of Christ: "Brothers and sisters, if someone is caught in a sin, you who live by the Spirit should restore that person gently. But watch yourselves, or you also may be tempted. Carry each other's burdens." Condemnation of unbiblical theological beliefs or immoral behavior must be done gently. But both Jesus and Paul urge us to do it—even to the point of excluding the unrepentant person from the body of believers (Matt. 18:17; 1 Cor. 5:1–5).

A commitment to biblical truth in our time means that we must dare (gently, lovingly, but clearly) to identify and reject theological error and immoral behavior. Knowing that our theological and ethical beliefs could be mistaken means that we will listen carefully to those who disagree. We will always be ready to listen to other views. But awareness of the possibility that we might be wrong should not—dare not—immobilize us and prevent us from taking clear stands on theological and ethical issues. After we have done our best biblical exegesis, theological reflection, and dialogue with other Christians, we rightly act on those beliefs and lead churches that disciple people committed to those beliefs.

Gentleness and Truth

Always, of course, Jesus's approach to the woman caught in adultery must be our model. Jesus rejected the angry call to stone her. There is no doubt that the woman felt Jesus's love for her in a powerful way. But in the end, he gently told her to stop sinning (John 8:11).

My prayer for this generation of young evangelicals is that you will apply Jesus's combination of gentleness and truth. A passion for biblical fidelity never justifies harshness. But love dare not trump truth.

By all means, learn from postmodernism the many complex ways that our ideas and beliefs are shaped by our social setting. Be aware that even our best efforts to understand God's truth are partial and imperfect. But dare to affirm and live out the historic Christian affirmation that moral and theological truth exist—precisely because they are grounded in God.

Response by Ben Lowe

Ron is right. Many in my generation are wary of truth claims. We don't want to be unnecessarily exclusive or offensive. And we're uncomfortable with the arrogant and aggressive reputation Christians have gotten for advocating for our beliefs. We've often handled truth poorly in the past. We're eager to become more thoughtful and charitable moving forward, both for our own sake and for those who have to put up with us.

I understand that there are also those in my generation unsure about the existence of moral and theological truth altogether. I don't identify with this position, however. I believe that truth exists and that we have the opportunity to seek it as best we can in community and through God's revelation and the Holy Spirit's illumination. But truth is not up for us to define. It exists beyond us and is found in and determined by God.

My hope is that we will become better at holding to what we believe is true without, to put it plainly, being jerks about it. It's not always easy to balance being tolerant with being steadfast, but it's possible. Although, of course, while each of us has the freedom to choose what we believe, that doesn't mean we're necessarily right.

On that note, history is replete with examples of Christians who were confident but dramatically wrong about many things. We Christians infamously fought to maintain that the sun revolves around the earth (oops), and many also used the Bible to defend the practice of slavery. Then there are the battles being waged on all manner of doctrinal positions, whether it's Calvinism versus Arminianism, premillennialism versus amillennialism, or other contested issues such as infant baptism, speaking in tongues, divine healing, the age of the earth, and the list goes on.

Nobody thinks they're wrong—if they did, one hopes they'd change positions—but not everyone can be right. None of us currently has a lock on the truth.

Growing up in evangelical Christianity, I saw the world in black and white. There was right and there was wrong. There was truth and there was falsehood. I also thought that we could simply read and apply the whole Bible literally. I did not understand the challenges of exegesis and hermeneutics, and the importance of literary genres or authorial intent. Of course, this left me confused and troubled by certain parts of Scripture. But I assumed that even if I didn't know all the answers, there were smarter people who did. Life was simpler back then.

As I grew older, however, this simplistic worldview became less and less tenable. Reality, I learned, is often not black and white. There's a lot of gray in our understanding of God and the world. As Ron notes, because of both our natural finitude and the distortions of sin, things aren't as clear-cut as we sometimes like to pretend. God has gifted us with intelligence and revelation unparalleled across the rest of creation. It's amazing what we've learned and uncovered. But we're still very much fallible and limited creatures. There's much we don't know, and what we do know, we often glimpse only dimly. As the apostle Paul puts it: "For now we see only a reflection as in a mirror; then we shall see face to face. Now I know in part; then I shall know fully, even as I am fully known" (1 Cor. 13:12).

We need to come to terms with the tension that results from living in a complex and confusing world, where what is true and right is often not clear or straightforward. My upbringing in church did not prepare me well to deal with this reality. How can we move forward more faithfully in both what we hold to as truth as well as how we stand for these beliefs? I offer five suggestions.

1. Cultivate Humility

We've often been haughty and closed-minded about our doctrine and worldview. We've not been self-critical enough and have tended to view questions and criticisms as threats. Given all our mistakes, limitations, and blind spots, however, shouldn't Christians be far more humble today, particularly about the new ideas we promote as well as the historical debates that lack resolution?

Being humble is not the same as giving up on objective truth or walking away from our beliefs, even the exclusive ones. But it does mean having a more grounded view of our human fallibility. It means being honest about the areas we aren't as sure about. It means being willing to trust God in these gray areas instead of trying to generate clarity or certainty where they don't yet exist.

Cultivating humility empowers us to strive for a better balance between doctrinal discipline and being open to considering other thoughtful perspectives, and potentially growing from them. And it means not being so fearful about ideas that don't line up with our own worldview. Fear can easily cause us to miss opportunities for deepening our understanding and maturing our faith.

2. Pursue Understanding

Created in the image of God, we have a remarkable capacity to learn and grow. There's so much truth and understanding available to us, both through studying God's natural revelation (the created world) and God's special revelation (the divinely inspired Scriptures). With the Holy Spirit's gifts and illumination, and grounded in our history and communities, we can continue to expand our knowledge and unravel great mysteries.

This is good but hard work, and it takes ongoing intentionality and commitment. Are we willing to put in the needed effort here? Of course, we can't all be experts in everything, so we'll need to be unafraid of asking questions and trusting one another's expertise to round out our own. Toward that end, we'll also need to better value good science and research. Evangelical Christians have often not been known for valuing science or the life of the mind.[14] If all truth is God's truth, however, we'll need to be open to finding truth wherever it exists, especially when that's outside the church.

3. Distinguish the Essentials

Not every hill is worth dying on. On one hand we need to avoid being tossed about constantly as if there were no knowable foundation on which to anchor our lives. On the other hand, we need to prayerfully determine what the core essentials of our faith are and what topics/issues are more secondary.

For instance, the three main branches of Christianity—Catholic, Orthodox, and Protestant—all affirm the Apostles' Creed as being essential for orthodoxy. As part of that, Christians believe that God created the earth and everything in it. How and when he did that, however, is more open to debate. The same is true of our eschatology. Christians believe that Christ is coming back one day, but there are multiple schools of thought on exactly what that will look like. You can be a premillennialist, an amillennialist, or a postmillennialist and still be a Christian. As the ancient and well-known saying goes: "in essentials unity; in nonessentials liberty; and in all things charity."

4. Disagree Graciously

Speaking of charity, Christians have often struggled to relate well with those with whom we disagree or those who hold what some of us define as heterodox views. This is a significant factor behind why we have so many denominations today, not that denominations are all bad. At the end of the day, it's God's truth, not ours, and it's ultimately his to both reveal and defend.

Christianity in general, and evangelicalism in particular, has a track record of being reactionary, exclusive, and harsh. I once sat through a sermon that was entirely about identifying and castigating "modern-day heretics" in the American church. I generally agreed with the preacher's concerns over the theology of the so-called heretics he named, but I found his tone and approach unconstructive and inappropriate—it was more of a one-sided public rant than a sermon. It's not that we shouldn't disagree when needed, but we sure could be a lot more loving and gracious about it.

We all want to be treated well by those with whom we disagree, so let's do to others what we'd like done to us. Yes, heresy can be a dangerous and misleading problem that requires addressing. But, as Ron wrote, "Condemnation of unbiblical theological beliefs or immoral behavior must be done gently." It's more than about just being right. It's also about being loving. It's more than about winning a debate. It's also about being winsome.

5. Live It Out

Finally, what's the use of knowing truth if we don't live it out? Too often, our beliefs as Christians don't consistently affect how we act. For instance, if we believe God created the world, then wouldn't more of the church eagerly treat it with care? Or if we really believe Christ's call to deny ourselves, take up our cross, and follow him (see Luke 9:23), then why do so many of us focus so much on accumulating wealth, social status, and worldly comforts? Moral and theological truths are not just abstract ideas to intellectually affirm, they're meant to define our lives and direct our lifestyles.

As we live out our beliefs, we remember that, at the end of the day, they should point us to God. The surest way we will know truth, and know what to do with it, is to completely surrender to the source of all truth. To pursue truth, we pursue God. We don't just go through religious motions or traditions. Instead, we are invited to follow after Christ with our whole being. And we trust that God gives us the ability to know and learn everything we need to in order to be faithful to this calling.

DISCUSSION QUESTIONS

1. Can you think of an area of doctrine or worldview in which you agree that we evangelicals have been too "haughty and closed-minded"? How should we cultivate humility in this specific area?

2. Can you think of any areas where we can find "God's truth" outside the church? What would be an example of how you are "pursuing understanding" in this area?

3. It often seems that there are many hills on which many Christians are willing to die—issues that are considered nonnegotiable matters over which we are willing to cut others off or be cut off. How do you feel about this, and are any of these nonnegotiable matters unnecessary or misplaced?

4. In your own life and church, what's one area in which you are striving to "disagree graciously" with people who view

you as holding a wrong view? Or with people whom you view as holding wrong views? How are you doing in this?

5. Imagine that someone were to listen to you for an entire month. What would that person say is the biblical truth you are most outspoken about? Now, would you say that this truth is something you are primarily trying to put into practice in your own life? Or is it something you mostly want other people to do?

4

Will You Keep Your Marriage Vows Better Than My Generation?

RON SIDER

I ask you, my young friends, will you beg God to give you the wisdom and strength to keep your marriage vows (if you choose to marry)?[1] Will you do vastly better than my generation of evangelicals in keeping your marriage vows of lifelong faithfulness? I feel deep sorrow when I reflect on the pain and agony that so many evangelicals of my generation have inflicted on their children because of widespread divorce in evangelical circles. When I hear that many of you hesitate to even get married because of the conflict and hell you witnessed as your parents fought and divorced, I weep. With all of my heart, I want to assure you that you need not repeat that tragedy. In the power of the Risen Lord, it is quite possible to marry, keep your marriage vows, grow together over the years, and love each other just as deeply after fifty or sixty years of marriage as on your wedding night.

It is not surprising that a generation that experienced the sexual revolution of the 1960s engaged in widespread sexual promiscuity and escalating divorce. Popular music, movies, and television belittled marriage and encouraged adultery and divorce. Even very liberal people like Sylvia Ann Hewlett and coauthor Cornel West acknowledge this: "The overwhelming message from progressive liberal folks in Hollywood is *Who needs a husband to have a child?*"[2] In the ten years after no-fault divorce laws became the norm across the country in the late sixties, the divorce rate doubled. Divorcing parents tried to tell themselves that their actions would not harm their children.

The Data

But the facts prove otherwise. In subsequent decades, sociological study after sociological study has demonstrated how devastating divorce (and single parenthood) is for children. Professors at Princeton University and the University of Pennsylvania discovered in a huge, sophisticated study that boys who grow up without their fathers are twice as likely to go to jail as boys growing up with both of their parents. For every year a boy lived apart from his father, the likelihood of going to prison increased by 5 percent.[3]

Children in divorced or single-parent families are two to three times more likely than children living with both of their parents to have emotional and behavioral problems. They are more likely to have academic trouble, drop out of high school, become pregnant as teenagers, abuse drugs, commit crimes, and become mentally ill. Eighty percent of all adolescents in psychiatric hospitals come from broken homes. Three out of four teen suicides occur in single-parent homes. Seventy percent of the juveniles in state reform institutions grew up in fatherless homes.[4]

Nor are stepfathers a good substitute. Boys with stepfathers are 2.9 times more likely to go to jail than boys living with their biological mother and father. In fact, delinquency rates are lower for boys living with a single mother than for boys living with their mother's boyfriend or new husband.[5]

Divorce also increases the likelihood of children experiencing poverty. After their parents divorce, children are almost twice as likely to live in poverty. Only 12 percent of children living with both parents are in poverty, but 31 percent of children with divorced parents live in poverty.[6]

Writing in *The New York Times*, David Popenoe summarized the sociological data bluntly: "I know of few other bodies of data in which the evidence is so decisively on one side of the issue: on the whole for children, two-parent families are preferable."[7]

One would have thought that evangelical homes would have resisted the societal trend toward easy, widespread divorce. Evangelicals claim to follow Jesus, not societal norms. One of the most central affirmations of evangelicals is that Christians obey biblical teaching. And the Bible is very clear about divorce.

Divorce was easy (for men) in Jesus's day. But Jesus sharply narrowed the basis for legitimate divorce. Citing the Creator's design in Genesis that a "man will leave his father and mother and be united to his wife, and the two will become one flesh," Jesus concluded: "Therefore what God has joined together, let no one separate" (Matt. 19:5–6). And when the Pharisees reminded Jesus that the Mosaic law specifically allowed a husband to give his wife a certificate of divorce and send her away (Deut. 24:1), Jesus set aside Moses's permission for divorce: "I tell you that anyone who divorces his wife, except for sexual immorality, . . . and anyone who marries a divorced woman commits adultery" (Matt. 5:32).[8]

The last book of the Old Testament is equally clear: "I hate divorce, says the LORD, the God of Israel" (Mal. 2:16 NRSV).

Tragically, this clear biblical teaching was not enough to keep many evangelicals from succumbing to the surrounding culture. Studies show that evangelicals get divorced at about the same rate as everyone else!

Actually, evangelicals get divorced at a slightly higher rate than the general population. The massive data in the General Social Survey (a highly respected, nationwide survey conducted by the National Opinion Research Center at the University of Chicago since 1972) show that from 1980 to 2009, the divorce rate among evangelicals was 1–3 percent higher than the general population.[9] Furthermore, over the same thirty years, evangelicals divorced at a substantially higher rate than mainline Protestants and Catholics. The rate for evangelicals was 40 percent; whereas the rate for mainline Protestants was 35 percent, and that for Catholics was 32 percent.[10]

Brad Wilcox is a Princeton-trained Christian sociologist who specializes in family issues. After studying two large sets of national data, he concluded: "Compared with the rest of the population, conservative Protestants are *more* likely to divorce." He has also pointed out that in the southern United States, where conservative Protestants make up a higher percentage of the population than elsewhere in the United States, divorce rates are higher.[11]

Conclusions from the Data

It is crucial, however, not to conclude from these statistics that Christian faith makes no difference in people's lives or is even negative. When one compares active Christians (i.e., those who attend a religious service on a weekly basis) with nonactive Christians (those who attend much less frequently), the contrast is striking. Whereas 49 percent of nonactive evangelicals get divorced, only 31 percent of active evangelicals do. For Catholics, nonactive persons have a divorce rate of 39 percent, whereas the rate for active Catholics is only 21 percent. And with mainline Protestants, the percentages are 39 percent versus 26 percent. Furthermore, Americans with "no religion" divorce at a much higher rate (50 percent) than Catholics, mainline Protestants, and evangelicals.[12]

But certainly one cannot rest comfortably with the fact that those who profess no religion divorce at a somewhat higher rate (50 percent) than Christians (who range from 32 percent for Catholics to 40 percent for evangelicals). What a tragedy that even 31 percent of evangelicals who attend church at least once a week still get divorced.

I do not mean to be harsh and unloving to those who have experienced the pain of divorce. My wife, Arbutus, was a marriage and family therapist for more than twenty years. I know from many conversations with her that there are some tough, complicated situations where it is hard to discern the right path.[13] Sometimes one's spouse simply walks away and refuses attempts to renew the marriage. But so many married couples give up so easily. Rather than work through the problems that inevitably trouble even the best of marriages, so many just run from the marriage—and then often discover the same problems in their next marriage.

I know from personal experience—and I have been married to Arbutus Lichti Sider now for fifty-four years—that lifelong marriage not only requires attention and work but also leads to deep, abiding joy.

Even before we were formally engaged, we talked easily about almost everything. After marriage, we talked together about everything in our lives and made our decisions together. Nevertheless, I simply assumed the validity of the "soft patriarchy" that my dad and mom modeled. They loved each other dearly and made decisions together, but Dad was clearly in charge and had the last word.

By the early 1970s, however, "biblical feminism" was emerging in evangelical circles. I helped organize the event that issued the 1973 Chicago Declaration of Evangelical Social Concern. And that document called for "mutual submission." In 1975, Arbutus attended the Washington Conference of the Evangelical Women's Caucus and came back with a much deepened understanding of how vigorously Jesus had challenged male prejudice and affirmed the full equality of women. She told me she had "fallen in love with Jesus again." But she also said: "This is so important for me that I fear that if we do not go on this journey together, we will grow apart, and I don't want that to happen." We agreed to journey together.

I was theoretically and theologically committed to the full equality of women. But that did not mean I did my share of washing the dishes and cleaning the toilet! It took time for me to grow toward practicing what I preached. As we struggled, grew, and changed, we were determined to remain faithful to Jesus and biblical revelation. Over the years a strong engagement with Christians for Biblical Equality helped us do that.[14] I am certain that the mutual submission that we increasingly and more fully embraced has been a significant factor in the joy that we have experienced through fifty-four years of marriage.

But it did not mean the absence of struggle and pain.

When we approached our fortieth birthdays after about eighteen years of happy marriage, Arbutus and I experienced a very difficult time. A nasty temper that had not been there before began to explode in me. We had many angry arguments. Arbutus begged me to go together to seek the help of a Christian family therapist. But I proudly resisted, arguing that the other couples in our house church needed counseling more than we did. (That may have been true!) Ironically, I was preparing for a series of three lectures for a national peace conference precisely at the time when my explosive temper was at its worst. More than once, I had a big fight with Arbutus over the weekend and then sat down on Monday morning to try to write one of my lectures on peace! I remember praying: "Dear Father, I know this is awful but please forgive me and help me complete this lecture today because I have only a short time to finish it."

Finally, I agreed with Arbutus that on my way home from the peace lectures, I would visit our closest friends and talk about our troubled marriage. Thank God, they lovingly but firmly warned me that unless I agreed to get counseling for our marriage, we would end up in a terrible situation. So I came home and told a very happy Arbutus that I was finally ready to have us seek professional help.

Those six months were tough. We struggled hard. Fortunately, our strong commitment to obey our Lord Jesus—including his command against divorce—meant that we never seriously considered abandoning the marriage. And our excellent marriage counselor helped us understand ourselves and each other much better. We learned to taste each other's feelings— he told us to literally put on each other's shoes as we prayed for each other. He helped us learn to state the other's views in a way that the other agreed showed real understanding. We learned that it was really okay for us to disagree on various issues—even theology.

For decades now, we usually retire to bed together when both of us are home. We usually spend a little time praying together in each other's arms. (We wrote a short piece about "Devotional Snuggling"![15]) We have tried to practice the principle of not going to sleep angry at each other. We have usually—although not always—managed to do that. It is hard to stay angry if you are lying in each other's arms praying!

The Three Cs

As I have reflected on what keeps a marriage strong, growing, and joyful over a lifetime, I have come to emphasize three Cs: *covenant*, *cross*, and *community*.[16] Covenant must replace contract; the cross of self-sacrifice must replace personal self-realization; and individualism must give way to community so that the church can offer powerful communal support to marriages and families.

First of all, *covenant*. Jesus's teaching in Matthew 19 conveys the biblical understanding of marriage covenant: "What God has joined together, let no one separate" (v. 6). Let no person tear apart this divinely established covenant of lifelong unity. Marriage is not just for good times; it is for bad times too. It is "for better, for worse, for richer, for poorer, in sickness and health, till death do us part."

We grasp the full force of Jesus's teaching only when we remember that in first-century Palestine, divorce was easy—at least for a man. Jesus explicitly sets aside the Mosaic law and returns to the Creator's original plan. "It was because you were so hard-hearted that Moses allowed you to divorce your wives, but from the beginning it was not so" (Matt. 19:8 NRSV). In Jesus's dawning kingdom, the disciples of Jesus should and can keep marriage vows the way the Creator originally intended.

Frequently, Jesus relaxed rigid ethical rules of his time. But here in the case of divorce he did just the opposite. To be sure, he permitted divorce in the one case of marital unfaithfulness (Matt. 19:9). But his teaching clearly, pointedly excludes divorce for the vast majority of reasons people today abandon their spouses.

Carol Schreck

*Emeritus Associate Profes-
sor of Marriage and Family,
Palmer Theological Seminary*

Peter Schreck

*Emeritus Professor of Pas-
toral Care and Counseling,
Palmer Theological Seminary*

Is it exaggerating to claim that marriage is the relationship that best enables two people to be for and with each other mutually and permanently? Think for a moment. Where else does one person promise to love another no matter what, to "hang in" no matter what, to stay faithful no matter what? But truth be told, all too often such promises express the ideal, while life presents reality. And we know the consequences—unfulfilled people in unhappy marriages, divorce rates that hover near 50 percent, and alternatives to marriage increasing in popularity.

And still people marry—even marry again! Young people marry later (often because of fear) but still admit to the longing for a soul mate. Marriage still attracts. Longings for unconditional love, for a life partner, and for a safe emotional harbor have not waned because we are inherently relational. It is no accident; we were *created* for relationship by virtue of being made in the image of a relational God who makes and keeps covenant marked by steadfast love and faithfulness. Marriage reflects that.

Love is virtually synonymous with marriage, though "love" needs some elaboration. Certainly marital love includes the emotional "in love with each other" and the erotic "making love" of sexuality (in fact, intercourse really *makes love* only within the relational safety of steadfast love and faithfulness). But the love sought and given in marriage also embraces functional dimensions such as equitably sharing the tasks of daily life and actively fostering the other's growth (not to be confused with being responsible for the other). These aspects of marital love underscore the Creator's assessment that it was "not good for the man to be alone" (Gen. 2:18) and make evident that marriage is God's idea, graciously instituted for the mutual well-being and growth of both spouses. A marriage rich in romantic, erotic, and functional love also provides the best environment for the creation, nurture, and growth of children.

As Christians we also want our marriages to serve as outposts of God's grace and presence in our world. If we do that well, those around us will notice and say, "Behold, how they love one another."

Jesus's standard is high. Large parts of the modern church flatly defy Jesus's teaching. Christians cannot hope to restore the family unless we are ready to return to the Creator's design. Are Christian couples today ready to follow Jesus rather than conform to the world? It will not be easy, but it is the only way to restore the family and recover the deepest joy in marriage.

At some point, the storms of life will roar through every marriage like a raging tornado. At that point, the best protection against giving up is to be committed without reservation for the rest of one's life—"till death do us part." If that is clear, then we will struggle, we will cry, we will pray and trust God to bring us through.

The world has a cheap substitute for Christian marriage covenant. It is called contract. Sometimes the contract is explicit. Some couples approaching marriage actually work out a written contract. They agree on what each party will do.

If the one party breaks the agreement and fails to keep their promises, then it is okay to dissolve the marriage because it is just a contract. More often the contract is implicit. We do not say explicitly that it is just a contract, but it is. We say, "Let's try it. Let's see if it works. Let's see if it feels good. Let's see if it meets my needs." Behind those words, of course, is the hidden assumption of contract and the lie that self-realization should be our highest priority. If the other party does not meet my needs, then the contract is broken. If I do not enjoy self-fulfillment, then the contract is off.

Society's limited marriage contract is not Christian covenant. It is the devil's cheap substitute. It is a fraud, a trick. Satan, of course, sells it to us with slick language and big promises. He says it brings freedom. He argues: "Society changes; you change; how on earth can you make a lifelong covenant?" I want to shout to my children, to all of our children, to all of us: "Let us not be deceived by Satan's lousy substitute. Let us choose unconditional, solemn covenant made in the presence of the living God rather than a limited liability contract. In God's name, let us choose Christian partners who share that biblical understanding. And then, let's keep our vows, no matter what the world says and does." That is the only foundation strong enough to bring us the deep joy of continuing growth and lasting love over a lifetime of mutual submission and sacrifice. Covenant—biblical covenant before God—is the foundation of Christian marriage.

The second C is *cross*. Anybody who has been married a few months knows there is pain as well as joy in marriage. We are all proud, petty, selfish sinners. We hurt each other, and then, silly and stupid as we are, we try to cover it up or blame our spouse. We refuse to say we are sorry. Even in the best of marriages, we hurt each other deeply. Finally, there is only one solution for that. It is a costly solution. It is the mystery at the heart of the gospel. It is the cross. It is costly forgiveness.

Ephesians 5 says that husbands should love their wives the way Christ loved the church. (I'm sure Christ wants wives to do the same for their husbands.) How does Christ love the church? He died for us. He put aside short-term self-fulfillment and embraced the agony of Roman crucifixion. Why? Not because we are so good. He did it because he loved us so much that he gladly sacrificed himself to bring us unconditional forgiveness.

That kind of costly love is absolutely essential for lifelong, joyful marriage. Betrayal, sin, and anguish will invade every marriage. At that point, there is one good option and two bad ones.

One misguided choice is to let resentment and anger take control. Eventually that will destroy the relationship.

Another wrong choice is to pretend it really does not matter much. "Aw, shucks. It was nothing. In fact, I have already forgotten it." That, of course, is a lie. Pretense and cheap grace simply cannot bring about reconciliation and restore intimacy.

Costly forgiveness is the only choice that really works. That is the way of the cross. Pain, betrayal, selfishness, and sin in marriage do matter. They hurt like crazy. They tear us apart. Costly forgiveness responds to the hurt in marriage the same way that God responds to sin. Sin is damnably serious. But at the cross, God embraces the punishment we deserve because God loves us in spite of our sinful failures.

That kind of costly forgiveness is the only way to stay happily married for a lifetime. When betrayal comes, we need to deal with it. We need to face clearly the full agony of this vicious javelin thrust into our hearts. Sin needs to be confessed. Genuine repentance is essential. Then in time, by God's grace, we can also add: "Because I love you, I accept the pain of your betrayal and I forgive you." That is the only way for husbands and wives to achieve reconciliation and joy after betrayal. You cannot pretend that you have not been hurt. You cannot wish it away. You can only embrace the pain and forgive. As repentance and forgiveness strengthen and reinforce each other, healing and reconciliation slowly grow.

How often do we need to embrace the cross in our marriages? Husbands are to love their wives and wives are to love their husbands as Christ loves the church. How often does Christ forgive you? Seventy times seven and seventy times seven. How many times has Christ forgiven you in the past year? In the last ten years? In the last fifty years? That is the way that we need to go on forgiving our husband or our wife.

That does not mean spouses should overlook persistent patterns of abuse and other sinful behavior. Rather than becoming codependent enablers, we must confront wrong. When separation becomes necessary, the Christian community should walk with both parties, nurturing repentance, healing, and eventually reconciliation.

Costly forgiveness is closely related to covenant. The cross means never giving up. As long as we live, Christ stands before us offering forgiveness. God does not say, "I have had enough of you. I have had enough of your failures, stupidity, unfaithfulness, and sin." As long as we live, God stands there pleading: "I want to give you another chance." Taking the way of the cross in our marriages, loving our spouses as Christ loved the church, means not giving up, even in the difficult, painful times.

This is not, I hasten to add, a recipe for agony and masochism. It is the only way to healing and joy. It is the only way to lasting happiness in marriage. Since pain and failure will always come, even in the best of marriages, the only way to restoration and wholeness is costly forgiveness. The cross is central to Christian marriage.

The third crucial element Christian marriages need is genuine *community* in the church. Young people may think, "All this sounds scary. The demands seem very high." That is true. It is also true that the rewards are even greater. But when a life-long commitment seems hard, Christians remember that we are not alone. In addition to the daily presence of the Spirit, Christians enjoy the love and support of the church. All of the other brothers and sisters in the body of Christ promise to help us. That is why we have church weddings rather than just going off by ourselves to elope. The wedding covenant is not merely a solemn pledge between God and two persons. It is also a communal vow witnessed by our brothers and sisters in Christ. By attending the wedding, they all pledge to help us in our marriage covenant.

In Christ's body, if one suffers, all suffer. If one rejoices, all rejoice (1 Cor. 12:26). That means celebrating weddings and fiftieth anniversaries together in the body of Christ. It also means standing together in the tough times. That is what we promise every young couple we watch walk down the aisle to be married in the church. We are responsible for one another's marriages. Everybody in a congregation is responsible if somebody's marriage fails. Did we pray or gossip? Did we cry or silently sneer? Did we gently counsel them to hold on or did we stay coldly silent? Did we offer costly help or let them struggle alone?

There are numerous ways that the Christian community could strengthen marriage and family. We need much more teaching for our children and youth about the beauty and joy of lifelong commitment in marriage. We need more premarital counseling. I wish that every church would announce that it will not marry anyone unless they have gone through several months of Christian marriage counseling. We also need better postmarital counseling. We need to share our marriage struggles in small fellowship groups and encourage one another to get counseling when necessary.

Satan is a clever liar. He says marriages used to last because people had no other option. They hated each other, lived parallel lives, and only stayed together because of custom. That is partly true and partly false. But Christian community provides a solution to the truth in this charge. I do not believe God wants us to endure continuing agony in our marriages. A church that genuinely understands what it means to be the body of Christ will find ways to help one another work at the pain, the failures, the hurts in each of our marriages. Unless the church is ready to invest large amounts of money and time in helping its members discover new joy and wholeness in their marriages, it should not criticize the world or pretend that it has an alternative to the sexual and marital tragedy all around us. But the church today does know a better way. We know that lasting, fulfilling marriage starts with biblical covenant, is renewed by costly forgiveness, and is strengthened by the warm, supportive embrace of loving sisters and brothers in Christ.

God's way for marriage works better! It is better for our children. It is better for the church. It is better for society. And wonderfully, it is also better for ourselves. I am absolutely convinced that when a wife and husband love, forgive, learn with, and grow together over a lifetime, they enjoy more happiness, joy, and, yes, self-fulfillment than those who choose divorce.

Nor should we overlook the evangelistic impact of joyful, wholesome Christian marriages. Just imagine the impact if even a quarter of today's Christians modeled joyful Christian marriages and families for the next two decades. There are few things that would have more evangelistic impact upon our world so full of broken homes.

I pray for tens of millions of Christian families whose joy and wholeness stand out in stark contrast to the surrounding darkness. In those homes husbands and wives know that the best thing they can do for their children is to love and care for each other. They take the time and invest the energy to communicate honestly, repent when they fail, forgive each other, grow together, find delight in each other, and submit to each other. They treasure family time more than promotions. They keep their vows even in the tough times. Their joyful, wholesome families demonstrate powerfully that the Creator's design for sex and marriage is finally the only way to enduring happiness, peace, and, yes, self-fulfillment.

Living models of that kind of joy and integrity would be a powerful witness in the midst of the pain in families today. Neighbors would watch carefully. Slowly, after making sure the joy is genuine, they would often seek the same wholeness and gladly embrace the same Lord.

In the next two decades, Christian marriage could become one of our most powerful means of evangelism. Today's hurting, broken families long for something better. We can offer them what they seek. But only if we first live it. Will enough Christians today follow Jesus rather than the world? Will enough Christians model such fidelity, joy, and wholeness in our marriages and families that the world will see and believe?

That can only happen family by family, person by person. Over the decades, God helping me, I have tried to treasure my wife and my children above work, money, and fame. They have been God's best gift to me after his Son.

One final word to my young friends who are not yet married. You cannot expect to live according to a biblical sexual ethic once you are married if you do not practice it now. If you are not willing now to behave sexually in a way that is biblically obedient, why do you think you will later keep your marriage vows and spare your children the agony of divorced parents? Can you look openly into the face of Christ and say: "Lord, I believe with all my heart that the way I am relating physically to others is pleasing to you"? Would you feel comfortable if you sensed the presence of the Lord on your dates? Please do not despair if you cannot say yes to those questions. Rather, accept God's overflowing forgiveness and ask the Risen Lord to empower you to live his way in the future.

For a couple years before our wedding, I carried a little note in my wallet promising God and myself that I would not engage in sex with Arbutus until we were married. That may sound like an old-fashioned idea coming from a seventy-six-year-old. (Yes, I am that old!) But the fact that we waited until marriage (and never engaged in sex with anyone else before or since) did not damage our psyches or spoil our sexual life. (And yes, even at seventy-six, we both find great delight in sex.)

My young friends, the Creator's way really works much better than today's sexual promiscuity. I believe with all my heart that your generation can, in the power of the Risen Lord, keep your marriage vows, experience joyous marriages, and thereby live winsome models of marital fidelity and happiness. I beg you, make that your goal, and then by God's grace do what it takes to reach it.

Response by Ben Lowe

How can we renew the valuable and sacred institution of marriage? How can my generation do better here when many of us have more bad examples than good ones, when our culture has such a warped view of relationships and happiness, and when so much attention is unhealthily focused on sex?

While some divorce studies are finding signs of hope, especially among more active Christians,[17] we've still got a lot to overcome in order to recover a robust and holistic view and practice of marriage. And I don't believe that the greatest threat to the biblical institution of marriage is same-sex marriage, as some evangelicals have chosen to fixate on. The greatest threat is that we're not doing marriage well. Period. We've so trivialized, individualized, and watered down the institution of marriage across the board that it often doesn't stand for much anymore. Growing up in broken homes, whether due to divorce or bad marriages, has caused considerable damage to many millennials and will continue to exert negative impacts for generations down the line. This is tragic.

Ron has addressed a lot of this, and he does so as someone who has been married for decades. In addition to being much younger, I'm also single. So my perspective is more as an outsider. But I've watched a lot of my friends in their marriages. And, as a pastor's kid, I've witnessed many troubled relationships and families. My parents are always careful to protect the confidentiality of the couples they counsel, but I'm aware (in general terms) of some of the issues they've dealt with over the years. So here are five lessons that stand out, in addition to what Ron has already shared, about how we can continue renewing the sacred covenant of marriage.

1. Separate Civil Marriage from Christian Marriage

When a couple gets married in church these days, there is usually a point in the service when the pastor says, "And now by the authority vested in me by God and by the state of (fill in the blank) . . ." I'm not as comfortable with having pastors double as agents of the state when performing what should be a sacred covenantal ceremony. While there's value to civil marriage in its own right, we should clearly distinguish it from the even greater meaning behind covenantal marriage. There are different standards and expectations for both, and conflating them for the sake of convenience is unhelpful.

2. Reject the Stereotypes and Power Struggles

Marriage is meant to be about thriving, not just surviving. It's not just about avoiding separation and divorce, but about building godly marriages. One of the obstacles to healthy unions is the stereotypical power struggle between husband and wife. It's regularly made fun of in television shows, movies, comedy routines, and even in Sunday sermons. We joke about men showing their wives who "wears the pants" in the relationship. Conversely, we also joke about men being "whipped" by their wives. There's a famous saying that "the man may be the head of the household, but the woman is the neck that turns the head." The reality, however, is that normalizing such manipulation and feeding into these and other gender stereotypes can be harmful—as is the gossip and badmouthing that often accompany such situations when husbands or wives get together and complain about their other half. Marriage is about mutual submission, sacrifice, intimacy, and trust. And these critical traits don't develop well in such a toxic environment.

3. Cultivate Community

While Ron has already flagged this, I've witnessed many couples get married and pursue intimacy with each other *at the expense of,* instead of in addition to, remaining connected in community. Marriage is often treated as being solely between the husband and wife and (one hopes) God. A healthier and more biblical approach, however, is that marriage is between the couple, God, *and their community.*

We desperately need to renew the role of the church and Christian community in strengthening the institution of marriage and supporting couples both before and after they get married. As a pastor, my father has a relatively firm policy here. He only marries couples who are part of the church he serves. He also requires them to go through an in-depth process of premarital counseling with church leaders who can continue to support them long after the wedding and honeymoon period are over.

Remaining connected in community—meaningful, accountable community that goes beyond mere socializing—can be a juggling act when married, especially if kids come along. It takes both intentionality and vulnerability to stay close and honest with key friends and mentors (without vulnerability turning into gossip, of course). But I've heard time and again from couples of all generations that it's worth it.

4. Get Serious about Divorce and Remarriage

The Bible speaks directly and repeatedly about divorce and remarriage among God's people. And the Gospels record Jesus teaching very strongly on this topic. In generations past, when divorces were less common, our churches spoke out equally strongly too. There were many factors behind the lower divorce rate back then and not all are good—sometimes abused or oppressed women felt they had nowhere to go, or couples stayed together for the sake of appearance but lived otherwise separate lives. With more Christians getting divorced, and more getting remarried, however, the church has grown much quieter here. It's become increasingly awkward and unpleasant to face these issues together. We don't want to judge others or be offensive, and we truly want to comfort and support our friends who are going through tough times.

There are legitimate grounds for divorce, and the church is called to offer love and healing for those who have been through such traumatic experiences. But we're also to be a holy community that calls one another to repentance and reconciliation. These are painful but not completely private matters, and they appropriately fall within the purview of the body of Christ. At the end of the day, we need to be faithful to who God is calling us to be, and how he is calling us to live. It's furthermore inconsistent and hypocritical that many of our evangelical churches today largely ignore addressing divorce and remarriage while taking a vocal stance against same-sex marriage.

5. Honor Singleness along with Marriage

There's a lot of social pressure to get married, and even more so among Christians. Many of us had or have friends in college who vowed to be married by the time they graduated (remember the "ring by spring" pressure?). Perhaps we were one of those people. As someone in the Asian American community, I face growing pressure to get married with each passing year. It's always well intentioned, and I don't hold it against anyone, but at the same time, such stress can lead us to make rash and unwise decisions. I've regrettably hurt others, and have been hurt as well, through caving in to the pressure to pursue relationships and try to make something work.

Many of our churches implicitly and/or explicitly elevate marriage above singleness, but there are no biblical grounds for this bias. In fact, if the apostle Paul has anything to say about it, and he does, then singleness has its advantages. It offers a way for us to serve God with greater, undivided devotion. Marriage, meanwhile, is permissible for those who can't control their lust, "for it is better to marry than to burn with passion" (1 Cor. 7:9). Whoa.

Obviously, the apostle Paul's words aren't the whole teaching on marriage in Scripture. But they are part of it. And I believe that if we want to renew the institution of marriage, then we will also need to renew the place of singleness and celibacy in our churches. Both states can be just as honoring to God because, at the end of the day, what ultimately defines us is not whether we are single or married but that we are redeemed as the children of God.

DISCUSSION QUESTIONS

1. How has divorce impacted your circle of friends? How have their divorces affected you?

2. Have you seen any great marriages in your circle of friends? Whether yes or no, how has this influenced you?

3. The concept of "contract" is very familiar to us, even in relationships. How do you understand the idea of "covenant" in the context of marriage?

4. In your own marriage, or in marriages you've seen, how has "costly forgiveness" served to keep husband and wife together?

5. Weddings are often held with the bride and groom surrounded by the body of Christ. Whether held in a church building or in a forest, the couple is therefore within "the church." But how does your own church community support that marriage once the wedding is over?

5

Will You Lead the Church to a Better Stance on Homosexuality?

A Better Vision

RON SIDER

I believe that younger evangelicals have an opportunity today to lead the way in a better approach to the painfully difficult topic of homosexuality—an approach that rejects much of recent evangelical practice but affirms the core understanding that almost all Christians have embraced for two thousand years.[1]

The widespread perception that evangelicals are hostile to homosexuals weakens our witness and even drives people away from Christ. Unfortunately, evangelicals are largely to blame for the widespread view that we are antihomosexual, homophobic, and hostile to gays. Too many of us have actually been homophobic. Too many of us have tolerated gay bashers. We were largely silent when bigots in the society battered or even killed gay people. We seldom dealt sensitively and lovingly with young people in our churches struggling with their sexual orientation. Some Christian parents rejected their children who announced that they were gay. Some Christian counselors caused great pain by conducting "conversion therapy" (it was largely unsuccessful) on young gay adults. Instead of taking the lead in ministering to people with AIDS, some of our leaders even opposed government funding for research to discover medicine to help them. Some even used the issue as an effective fund-raising tool. At times, we even had the gall to blame gay people for the tragic collapse of marriage in our society, ignoring the obvious fact that the main problem by far is that many of the 95 percent of the people who are heterosexual do not keep their marriage vows.[2] We have often failed to distinguish gay orientation from gay sexual activity. (There is nothing sinful in having a gay orientation where one is sexually attracted to a person of the same sex. Gay sexual practice, not gay orientation, is the important issue.[3]) If the devil had designed a strategy to discredit the historic Christian position on sexuality, he could not have done much better than what the evangelical community has actually done in the last several decades!

Some believe that the evangelical track record is so bad that we should just remain silent on this issue. But that would mean abandoning our submission to what finally, I believe, is clear biblical teaching. It would mean forgetting the nearly unanimous two-millennia-long teaching of Catholic, Orthodox, and Protestant Christians. And it would mean failing to listen to the vast majority of contemporary Christians (a majority of whom now live in the Global South).

I need to offer four preliminary notes.

First, when I use the word "gay" in this chapter, I am referring to same-sex orientation and relationships. I will sometimes (but not always) use the word "lesbian" to refer to female-female orientation or relationships. This chapter does not deal with other aspects of the LGBTQ (lesbian, gay, bisexual, transgender, and queer or questioning) discussion.

Second, I want to acknowledge clearly that this topic is painful and complicated. Many people with a gay orientation have experienced rejection and hostility in the church in a way that has been very painful. Some of these persons are Christians who remain in our churches. Others have rejected Christian faith—a result we all must grieve. Furthermore, the fact that the topic raises a whole host of issues—scientific, cultural, biblical, theological, ecclesiological, political—makes it very complicated.

Third, all human beings (even the best Christians most fully dedicated to biblical authority) can only "see through a glass, darkly" (1 Cor. 13:12 KJV). Our best understanding is always finite, limited, and imperfect. Only when we see the Lord face-to-face in the coming kingdom will we understand the full indisputable truth that only God now possesses. That does not mean that we should not assert and act upon what we believe is biblically and theologically correct (based on our best study and reflection). Jesus and the apostles command us to do that (Matt. 18:15–17; 1 Cor. 5:1–5). But it does mean that we must state our positions with grace, humility, and respect, and listen carefully to those we believe are wrong.

Fourth, this chapter deals almost exclusively with what the church should teach and practice. I do not discuss related issues of public policy (the 2015 decision by the Supreme Court has settled the legal question of same-sex marriage).[4]

Biblical Teaching

The primary biblical case against homosexual practice is not the few texts that explicitly mention it. Rather, it is the fact that again and again the Bible affirms the goodness and beauty of sexual intercourse—and everywhere, without exception, it is sexual intercourse between a man and a woman committed to each other for life.[5]

According to the creation account in Genesis, "Adam and his wife were both naked, and they felt no shame" (Gen. 2:25).[6] Their sexual attraction is good and beautiful. A whole book of the Bible—Song of Solomon—celebrates the sexual love of a man and woman. There are many, many Old Testament laws and proverbs that discuss the proper boundaries for sexual intercourse—and always it is between a man and a woman. Jesus celebrates marriage (John 2:1–11) and tightens the restriction on divorce—again always in the context of a man and a woman. Paul affirms the goodness of sexual intercourse by urging a husband and wife to satisfy each other's sexual desires (1 Cor. 7:1–7).

Both testaments use the relationship of husband and wife to describe God's relationship with his people: Yahweh's relationship to Israel in the Old Testament and Christ's relationship to the church in the New Testament.[7]

Again and again and again, the Bible discusses and affirms sexual intercourse. And always without exception, it is talking about a man and a woman.[8] It is within this context of widespread, unanimous affirmation of the goodness of sexual intercourse between a man and a woman committed for life that we must read the relatively few explicit biblical texts on same-sex practice.

Both Leviticus 18 and 20 contain a long list of prohibitions against certain kinds of sexual intercourse, including adultery, incest, bestiality, and lying "with a man as one does with a woman" (18:22; 20:13). The text says that God is driving out the inhabitants of Canaan (and giving the land to the people of Israel) because they practiced these "detestable" activities (18:24–28).

These prohibitions of same-sex practice in Leviticus say nothing about motives for or types of same-sex acts—e.g., gay rape or cult prostitution (common in Canaanite religion) or an older man with a boy. They simply—and unconditionally—prohibit all acts of sex between two males. The text says both are guilty and both must be punished.

Societies surrounding Israel were not nearly as universal in condemning same-sex activity. They often condemned it, but the punishment was less harsh than in Israel. And they also affirmed gay cult prostitution.[9] The unambiguous prohibition in the Leviticus texts, as Duke Divinity School scholar Richard Hays says, is "the foundation for the subsequent universal rejection of male same-sex intercourse within Judaism."[10]

Christians today still condemn most of the sexual acts forbidden in Leviticus 18 and 20, but not all—for example, having sex with one's wife during her monthly menstrual period. Furthermore, virtually all Christians today reject the penalty (death) in Leviticus for gay intercourse. The early Christians clearly rejected some parts of the Old Testament law while retaining others. So we must turn to the New Testament to see what it teaches about our topic.

The Pauline understanding is stated in Romans 1:24–27; 1 Corinthians 6:9; and 1 Timothy 1:10. Romans 1 contains the longest statement. In this chapter, Paul argues that even gentiles, who do not have God's special revelation in the Old Testament, are rightly condemned by God because they have rejected the clear revelation of God in creation. They exchanged the truth about God revealed in nature for a lie (embracing idols). God's punishment was to give "them over in the sinful desires of their hearts to sexual impurity" (v. 24).

Paul then cites the following illustrations:

> Because of this, God gave them over to shameful lusts. Even their women exchanged natural sexual relations for unnatural ones. In the same way the men also abandoned natural relations with women and were inflamed with lust for one another. Men committed shameful acts with other men, and received in themselves the due penalty for their error. (Rom. 1:26–27)

Thousands and thousands of pages have been written in recent decades to interpret this passage. Numerous authors in various ways argue that Paul does not mean (or at least contemporary Christians should not think) that all same-sex intercourse is wrong. Perhaps Paul only condemns pederasty (an older male with a boy was rather common in Greco-Roman culture), or cult prostitution, or uncommitted, temporary same-sex activity. Or perhaps Paul was thinking of the rather common Greco-Roman view in his day that it was a disgrace for a man to play the part of a woman because women were inferior to men.[11] But the text does not say any of those things. It seems to state a sweeping prohibition of same-sex intercourse—whether female with female[12] or male with male.

Paul seems to allude to Genesis as the norm for what is natural—that is, a man and a woman in sexual intercourse.[13] Romans 1:20 refers to the creation of the world. The words used in Romans 1:26–27 for male and female are the same ones used in the Greek translation of the Old Testament (the Septuagint) for male and female in Genesis 1.[14] Since Paul had just argued that the created world reveals who God is (1:18–21), it is certainly plausible to think that part of Paul's argument is that the creation itself calls for male-female intercourse but not same-sex intercourse.[15]

Greco-Roman moral philosophers who condemned same-sex behavior often used the phrase "contrary to nature" to describe gay intercourse. This language was especially strong in the Hellenistic Jewish writers of Paul's time. They often vehemently denounced all same-sex practice as contrary to nature. Hays, a New Testament scholar, says Paul "speaks out of a Hellenistic-Jewish cultural context in which homosexuality is regarded as an abomination and he assumes that his readers will share his negative judgment of it." Nature in Romans 1:26 and 27 means the created order.[16]

Paul's condemnation of same-sex intercourse appears to involve a comprehensive prohibition—thus both reflecting and reaffirming the teaching of Leviticus forbidding gay intercourse.[17]

Two other Pauline texts are relevant: 1 Corinthians 6:9 and 1 Timothy 1:10. As is the case with everything else on our topic, there is much debate about the meaning of the key words: *malakoi* and *arsenokoitai*.

In 1 Corinthians 6, Paul is responding to people in the Corinthian church who seem to think that traditional moral rules are no longer relevant. Paul rejects such thinking, declaring that "wrongdoers will not inherit the kingdom of God" (v. 9). Then he lists a number of actions that fall in this category: "Neither the sexually immoral nor idolaters nor adulterers nor men who have sex with men [*malakoi*, *arsenokoitai*] nor thieves nor the greedy nor drunkards nor slanderers nor swindlers will inherit the kingdom of God" (vv. 9–10).

It is tragic that most Christians talk much more about the sexual sins in Paul's list than sins like greed and slander. We must recover Paul's balance.

But what do the words *malakoi* and *arsenokoitai* mean? Hays points out that the word *malakoi* "appears often in Hellenistic Greek as pejorative slang to describe the 'passive' partners—often young boys—in gay activity."[18]

The other word, *arsenokoitai* (used again in 1 Tim. 1:10 in a similar list of sins), does not appear in any extant Greek text before Paul's use here in 1 Corinthians. This word combines two Greek words: *arsen* (the word for male) and *koitai* (the masculine plural noun of a word formed from the verb *koitē* [lying with]). Thus the meaning is a man lying with a man. It seems that only Jews and Christians used the compound word *arsenokoitai*.[19] And the compound word very likely emerged as they read the prohibition against homosexual practice in Leviticus 18:22 and 20:13 because precisely the same Greek words appear in the translation of these verses in the Septuagint (the Greek translation of the Hebrew Bible used in Paul's time). Pro-gay scholar Robin Scroggs has shown that Jewish rabbis used a parallel Hebrew phrase drawn from Leviticus 18:22 and 20:13 to refer to gay intercourse.[20] Therefore, as Hays says, "Paul's use of the term presupposes and reaffirms the holiness code's condemnation of homosexual acts."[21]

It is important to remember that Paul does not end his discussion with his list of sinful actions that prevent people from entering the kingdom. Instead, after noting that some Corinthian Christians had been such persons, Paul rejoices that they are now forgiven and transformed: "You were washed, you were sanctified, you were justified" (1 Cor. 6:11). Paul is not claiming complete sanctification. And he certainly is not commenting on our contemporary debate about whether persons with a long-standing same-sex orientation can exchange that for a heterosexual orientation (very few have, in spite of much effort). Rather, Paul is saying that the Holy Spirit works powerfully in the lives of Christians enabling them to turn away from former sins and resist ongoing temptation.

We can summarize the biblical material in this way. The most important fact is that in many places the Bible affirms the goodness of sexual intercourse—but only in the context of a marriage between a man and a woman. There are only a few texts that explicitly discuss same-sex intercourse. But they are unanimous in their prohibition of such action. Furthermore, the relative infrequency of discussion of such issues does not necessarily mean that they are unimportant. The fact that St. Paul mentioned incest only once does not mean he thought it was a minor or relatively harmless thing.

Hays is correct: "The early church did in fact consistently adopt the Old Testament teaching on matters of sexual morality, including homosexual acts."[22] Also, in both testaments, the texts clearly say (by the punishment prescribed or the result of the action) that the issue is very serious rather than something insignificant. The biblical teaching is unanimous.

Even writers who argue on hermeneutical grounds that the biblical teaching on same-sex practice is no longer normative for Christians today nevertheless acknowledge that the biblical teaching is universally negative. In his dialogue book with Robert Gagnon, pro-gay scholar Dan O. Via says, "Professor Gagnon and I are in substantial agreement that the biblical texts that deal specifically with homosexual practice condemn it unconditionally."[23] Pro-gay scholar John McNeill similarly notes that "wherever the Bible clearly seems to refer to homosexual activity, we must recognize a judgment and condemnation."[24] And Walter Wink, in an article in *Christian Century* advocating Christian acceptance of same-sex intercourse, bluntly acknowledges: "The Bible clearly considers homosexuality a sin. . . . I freely grant that. The issue is precisely whether that biblical judgment is correct."[25]

Hermeneutical Arguments

In spite of this biblical material, however, substantial numbers of Christians, including some evangelicals, offer hermeneutical

arguments to say that the church should affirm same-sex intercourse between gay or lesbian couples in committed, monoga-
mous, lifelong relationships. Not everything the New Testament teaches (e.g., head coverings for women) is still normative
today. We must examine some of the most important arguments
advanced to show either that Paul did not mean to condemn
lifelong same-sex relationships or that persuasive hermeneutical
arguments show that contemporary Christians rightly disagree
with St. Paul.

Argument 1: Paul Was Unaware of Lifelong Same-Sex Relationships

One of the frequent, substantive arguments is that the kind
of same-sex intercourse Paul knew and condemned is fundamentally different from the kind of same-sex relationships faithful Christians should accept today.[26] Typical gay intercourse in
Greco-Roman society was pederastic (a dominant older male
with a passive male youth). Not infrequently, it involved slavery
and rape. And sometimes it involved lascivious heterosexuals
who wanted sex with males in addition to sex with females.
The Bible, it is argued, only means to condemn pederastic and
exploitative gay intercourse. And in any case, the idea of a
lifelong exclusively same-sex orientation or a permanent gay
partnership ("marriage") was simply unknown in Paul's time.[27]

It is certainly true that the most common gay relationships
in Greco-Roman life were between men and boys (pederasty).
Other, even more exploitative relationships were not uncom-
mon. But Paul's discussion in Romans 1 says nothing about pederasty or exploitation. There is nothing in the text that suggests
that those are the reasons Paul prohibits same-sex intercourse.
Rather, it is "against nature" and contrary to the entire Jewish
understanding of God's will for sexual intercourse. And Paul

condemns both partners, not just a dominant or exploitative older male.

Nor is it convincing to say, as several do, that Romans 1:27 refers only to gay activity committed by males whose orientation is heterosexual but want the additional "thrill" of gay sex.[28] When Paul says, "Men also abandoned natural relations with women," he is not thinking in terms of a specific (heterosexual) man making a choice to engage in gay intercourse. Rather he is talking about the whole pagan culture that has abandoned what the creation tells us about God and "exchanged" (v. 23) it for idol worship; and similarly the pagan culture has abandoned what nature teaches us about sexual intercourse and "exchanged" (v. 26) it for same-sex intercourse. As Hays says, "The 'exchange' is not a matter of individual life decisions; rather it is Paul's characterization of the fallen condition of the pagan world."[29]

One of the major arguments of James Brownson's recent book *Bible, Gender, Sexuality* is that Paul (and the Greco-Roman world generally) simply did not know of the idea of a lifelong gay orientation or a permanent male-male sexual partnership. "The ancient world had no notion of sexual orientation."[30] Therefore contemporary Christians need not accept Paul's sweeping prohibition of all same-sex intercourse. In fact, however, there are clear examples in Greco-Roman literature of both a lifelong same-sex orientation and a permanent male-male sexual partnership.

In Plato's *Symposium* (which includes speeches at a banquet in 416 BC), Pausanias describes his love for Agathon, which had begun when Agathon (the younger man) was eighteen. But their gay relationship has continued for more than twelve years. Pausanias speaks strongly of the permanence of such a relationship: "For, I think, those who began from that moment [i.e., when the younger man begins to grow a beard] to fall in love with them are prepared to love in the expectation that they will be with them all their life and will share their lives in common; but not . . . go off and run away to another."[31]

In another speech by Aristophanes at the same banquet, we are told of the myth that originally, persons were binary beings of three types: a male-male type, a female-female type, and a male-female type. But Zeus split each pair in half. The result is that now each person from each type desires to reunite with his (or her) other half. Persons from a male-female binary type desire heterosexual partnerships. Women who come from a female-female binary type now "are inclined toward women." Men who came from a male-male binary type now "regard with affection men and rejoice when they lie down with and are locked together with men." Aristophanes says this same-sex orientation is permanent: "When they reach manhood, they become lovers of boys and are *not* inclined by nature toward marriage and the procreation of children." And not just the gay orientation but the male-male partnership is to be lifelong: "These are they who continue with one another throughout life."[32]

There are also other examples of lifelong erotic orientation in the ancient world. Ptolemy (an astrologer of the second century AD) said the configuration of the stars determined one's lifelong sexual orientation. Some astrological configurations produce an exclusively male-male orientation, others an exclusively lesbian one.[33] Ancient medical writers also sometimes spoke of people having a lifelong homoerotic identity.[34]

We cannot know, of course, whether St. Paul knew of these philosophical, astrological, and medical texts, but as a well-educated Roman citizen capable of quoting Greek authors, it is entirely possible that he did. In any case, it is simply not accurate to say that the idea of a lifelong same-sex orientation or of a long-term same-sex partnership was unknown in Paul's time. Thus one of Brownson's central arguments depends on historical inaccuracy.

Argument 2: Paul Was Misguided about Women and Procreation

Another argument used to claim that contemporary Christians rightly reject the biblical prohibition of same-sex intercourse is that the reasons people in Paul's day (and therefore presumably Paul himself) rejected same-sex intercourse are clearly misguided. Many ancients rejected gay intercourse because it belittled the supposed superior status of males versus females[35] and/or because it could not lead to procreation.

It is certainly true that many Greeks and Romans viewed women as fundamentally inferior to men. They saw men as strong and rational, and women as weak and ruled by passion; in intercourse the male is to be active, the female passive. Frequently those Greco-Romans who condemned gay intercourse did so explicitly because it meant that a male (who is supposed to be strong and active, not passive) plays the passive role of a woman. The very act defies the proper gender roles of superior male and inferior female. Similarly, in female-female intercourse, a woman must (disgracefully) take on the active role of a man. Contemporary Christians like myself who affirm the full equality and dignity of women find such an argument against same-sex intercourse totally unconvincing.

But Paul never uses this rather widespread ancient reason for opposing same-sex intercourse. He simply declares that all same-sex intercourse is wrong. The fact that some of Paul's contemporaries offered a misguided reason for rejecting same-sex intercourse says nothing about the reason for or validity of Paul's prohibition.

It is also true that many Greco-Roman writers as well as prominent Jewish thinkers (e.g., Philo and Josephus) condemned same-sex intercourse because it could not lead to children. (They also often condemned intercourse between a married man and his wife if it were not intended for procreation.) But again, Paul never hints at these arguments. His stated reason for marriage is to avoid sexual temptation, not to enable procreation (1 Cor. 7:2–5). And he writes positively of the ways that husbands and wives satisfy each other's sexual desires without any suggestion that the only valid reason for sexual intercourse in marriage is to bring children into the world. In fact, in amazing contrast with the preponderant view in his culture that the married woman must be passive in intercourse, Paul speaks of a total mutuality as wife and husband reciprocally yield to each other (1 Cor. 7:4).

In his condemnation of same-sex intercourse, Paul simply does not use the misguided arguments (common in his day) that all contemporary Christians should rightly reject.

Argument 3: Jesus Was Silent

What about the argument that since Jesus said nothing about same-sex intercourse and a great deal about loving everyone, we should conclude that he was at least indifferent about the issue?

We must remember Jesus's historical setting. All extant relevant evidence about Judaism in the two centuries before and after Jesus indicate that the Jews were unanimously and unequivocally opposed to same-sex intercourse. If Jesus had said anything that contradicted this contemporary Jewish consensus, it would have been shocking—and would have been remembered.

Nor is it the case that Jesus loosened contemporary sexual standards. Not just adultery but lust in one's heart is sin (Matt. 5:27–28). Jesus dramatically narrowed the grounds for legitimate divorce, setting aside the easy divorce privileges (for men) granted in the Mosaic law (Matt. 5:31–32; 19:3–9; see also Deut. 24:1–4).

Silence or infrequent mention of a topic is never proof that an issue is irrelevant or unimportant. It may simply mean that the societal consensus is so strong that no one asks a question about it. That is very probably why we have nothing from Jesus about same-sex practice. Jesus did not say anything directly about incest or bestiality, but hardly anyone would argue that therefore he did not consider them immoral.

What we do have from Jesus about sinners of all types including sexual sinners, however, is very important. The Pharisees denounced him for associating with sinners (Matt. 11:19). He was involved with women of ill repute (John 4:4–42). He refused to implement the Mosaic punishment (stoning) for adultery, suggesting that those without sin should cast the first stone. But after all the other men had slunk away, Jesus gently told the woman not to sin anymore (John 8:2–11).

Jim Daly

President and CEO, Focus on the Family

My friend Ron Sider hits all the right notes—standing solidly on biblical truth, exuding grace and love, and calling the church to be both a firm and winsome witness. Homosexuality may be the defining moral issue of our time, and it is becoming increasingly unpopular and uncomfortable to stand up for God's design for human sexuality. For that reason, it is vital that we do so now more than ever.

There are three key ideas to guide us here. First, all people—regardless of sexual attractions, identity, or behavior—are created in God's image. As a result, they all have great worth and are deserving of love and respect. Second, God's blueprint for human sexuality can be summed up in six short words: "male and female he created them" (Gen. 1:27). Let's proclaim with our words and our lives the wonderful truths that men and women are created to be both unique and complementary, that sex is a God-given gift intended to be shared exclusively within the bonds of marriage, and that marriage is for a lifetime.

Last, God's amazing grace enables us to live as he has called us. Christians who experience same-sex attractions do not have to act on those feelings, despite what the culture is telling them. Scores of men and women—through prayer, counseling, and the work of the Holy Spirit—have overcome unwanted desires. Many other equally faithful believers continue to struggle with those attractions, and yet remain committed to honoring God in this area of their lives.

Society today is experiencing confusion on these matters that would be unimaginable to previous generations. As our moral environment grows increasingly murky, Christians have a tremendous opportunity and responsibility to shine as beacons of grace and truth.

Jesus never condoned sin. But he modeled amazing love and concern for those ensnared by its destructive power. What a difference it would make if Christians today followed his example.

Argument 4: Same-Sex Attraction Is Biological

What if same-sex attraction is a genetic, inherited, unchangeable orientation? Does that mean it is morally right to engage in same-sex intercourse?

There is ongoing debate about the causes of same-sex orientation, but we can certainly agree that there are people who from their earliest experiences of sexual attraction are drawn only to those of the same sex. And the evidence clearly shows that most such people seem unable to change that attraction even after much effort, prayer, and anguish.

But the evidence is also quite compelling that some people inherit a predisposition to alcoholism that will likely overwhelm them if they start to drink. Some people (whether through their genes or socialization or both) are much more inclined to sex with children, incest, excessive overeating, and stealing. Surely Christians should not argue that every inborn trait is good and should be acted upon. The teaching of Romans is that there are many things that all of us are powerfully drawn to because of the fall that are sinful and must be resisted. Even if same-sex orientation is entirely due to genetic inheritance,[36] that in itself says nothing about whether same-sex intercourse is morally right.

Argument 5: Rejecting Same-Sex Relationships Is Similar to Condoning Slavery and the Oppression of Women

Another widely advanced hermeneutical argument for changing the historic Christian stance on same-sex intercourse builds on the way Christians today have moved beyond what the biblical text says about slavery and the role of women. The Old Testament explicitly allowed slavery, and neither Jesus nor any New Testament writer specifically condemned slavery (which was then a fundamental part of economic life in the Roman Empire) or called for its abolition. Christians today, nonetheless, agree that slavery is incompatible with biblical faith. Similarly, the inequality of women is clear in numerous Old Testament passages, and the New Testament does not offer any modern call for women's liberation. In fact, Paul says the husband is the head of the wife (Eph. 5:23) and women should "keep silent" in the church (1 Tim. 2:12 NRSV). And for many centuries, church practice relegated women to an inferior position—often citing a couple specific New Testament texts. But today, many Christians (and I am one of them) embrace a "biblical feminism" that affirms the full equality of women and men in church and society. If ongoing careful biblical exegesis, experience, and hermeneutical reflection (plus, one hopes, the guidance of the Holy Spirit) have rightly led Christians to abandon earlier views about slavery and women that they had claimed were grounded in the Bible, why then should not the same change be embraced with regard to committed, lifelong same-sex partnerships?

I consider this a serious argument that should not be dismissed lightly. But I think it is wrong for one fundamental reason. In the cases of slavery and women, there is a clear progression within the Bible itself from earlier acceptance of slavery and female inequality to strong indications that both are wrong. In the case of same-sex intercourse, on the other hand, there is not even a hint of a change within the canon. The prohibition in the New Testament is as clear as in the Old Testament.

The Old Testament does condone slavery. But even there, the biblical text places substantial limits on its practice and seeks to mitigate its severity (Deut. 15:12–14). The New Testament commends masters to treat their slaves with respect (Eph. 6:9). And when Paul sends the (new Christian) runaway slave Onesimus back to his Christian master, Philemon, Paul commands Philemon to treat his returned slave "no longer as a slave, but . . .

as a dear brother" (Philem. 16). When one understands the implications of that command, slavery becomes impossible!

The canonical progression in the case of women is even more striking. There is not a hint of inequality of women in the creation stories (Gen. 1; 2). But the fall led to enormous inequality as many Old Testament accounts illustrate—although even here, there are examples of women becoming powerful leaders (e.g., Deborah in Judg. 4:4–5:31). Jesus is dramatically different. He frequently ignored the rule that it was wrong for a man to appear in public with a woman. Even though a prominent rabbi said teaching the Torah (the first five books of the Bible) to a woman was like teaching her lechery, Jesus taught women theology (Luke 10:38–42).[37] Implementing the ancient prophecy that in the messianic time "your sons *and daughters* will prophesy" (Acts 2:17; cf. Joel 2:28), the early church had at least one female apostle (Rom. 16:7) and several prophets (Acts 21:9; 1 Cor. 11:5). Paul enunciated the amazing principle that in Christ "there is neither Jew nor Gentile, neither slave nor free, nor is there male and female, for you are all one in Christ Jesus" (Gal. 3:28).[38]

When contemporary Christians totally reject slavery and embrace the full equality of women, they are extending a trajectory clearly begun in the biblical canon. In the case of same-sex intercourse, on the other hand, there is nothing in the biblical canon that hints at such a change.[39]

Argument 6: Celibacy Is Impossible for Many and against God's Desire for Human Flourishing

If same-sex intercourse is wrong, then celibacy is the only option for Christians with a same-sex orientation. But many people argue that celibacy is both impossible for many and contrary to God's desire for human fulfillment. Many Christian proponents of same-sex practice argue, as does Dan Via, that a same-sex orientation is the "unifying center of consciousness" for a gay person.[40] Via also argues that God wants abundant life for everyone, "an aspect of which is bodily (sexual) life."[41] Or again: "Abundant life is such an all-embracing idea that it can include the specific actualization of whatever bodily-sexual orientation one has been given by creation."[42]

Several things must be said about this argument.

First, it would undoubtedly surprise Jesus and Paul (both celibate) who certainly did not think bodily sexual activity was necessary for abundant life.

Second, it is profoundly unbiblical to argue that one's sexual orientation is the defining aspect of one's identity (the "unifying center of consciousness" as Via insists). For Christians, our relationships to God and to the new community of Christ's church, not our sexual orientation, provide our fundamental identity. That is not to claim that our identity as men and women with particular sexual orientations is irrelevant or unimportant for who we are, but that sexual orientation dare never be as important to us as our commitment to Christ and his call to live according to kingdom ethics.[43]

Brownson argues, from Paul's teaching (1 Cor. 7:1–9) on marriage as a protection against sexual immorality (since many people cannot be celibate like Paul), that we ought to accept same-sex partners. Most people with a same-sex orientation, just like most people with a heterosexual orientation, lack the gift of celibacy. Therefore, Brownson argues, Paul's advice to heterosexuals ("They should marry, for it is better to marry than to burn with passion" [v. 9]) also applies to Christians with a same-sex orientation.[44] The church today should not expect them to be celibate.

But this argument that Christians with a same-sex orientation cannot be celibate ignores two facts. First, there are significant numbers of Christians with a same-sex orientation who do live celibate lives, and some speak movingly about how God's grace enables them to do that.[45] Second, it also ignores the fact that Christians over the centuries and still today call on large numbers of heterosexually oriented Christians to be celibate—and believe that it is possible in the power of the Spirit. This list includes younger widows and widowers; unmarried singles (many of whom would gladly marry if they could find a partner); and older people who have lost a spouse. The numbers of heterosexually oriented, unmarried people whom the church calls to celibacy are vastly larger than that quite small number (5 percent of the population at the most) that have a gay orientation. Do Christians who use this argument to promote Christian acceptance of same-sex intercourse also want us to conclude that the tens of millions of Christians who would like to marry but cannot find a partner obviously cannot practice celibacy and therefore should find a sexual partner? Hays is right: "The Bible undercuts our cultural obsession with sexual fulfillment."[46]

Brownson also offers a slightly different argument against the view that Christians with a same-sex orientation should be celibate. He claims that Jesus's teaching on lust means that the distinction between sexual orientation and sexual behavior is "ultimately untenable."[47] The *impulse* to sin must also be sinful, Brownson argues, because Jesus teaches that lust is actually already sinful adultery (Matt. 5:28). Brownson argues that if same-sex practice is sin, then, by the adultery analogy, the *impulse* toward same-sex practice (that is, a same-sex orientation) is also sin. Therefore the claim (that I and many others make) that having and acknowledging a same-sex orientation is not a sin (and that one sins only when one acts on this attraction) is finally wrong.

I think this argument depends on a misguided understanding of what Jesus means by lust. Obviously, we do not have a lengthy footnote from Jesus to explain exactly what he meant by lust. But I very much doubt that he intended to teach that any instinctive attraction to the physical beauty of a woman is like committing adultery. It is probably the case that many male heterosexuals (including this one) have a polygamous orientation that regularly prompts them to notice the physical beauty of women other than their wives in a way that goes beyond the way that the pure Jesus noticed the bodies of women. And this action in some important sense is a result of the fall. But Jesus, I am certain, means something different by lust. Lust is dwelling on the thought of another woman's beauty and continuing to think about acting on the attraction even though one never intends to commit physical adultery. I think that is what Jesus means by lust, which he condemns.

One can think of an analogy with many other "inclinations" or "orientations." Some have an inclination to alcoholism or pederasty or materialism. That initial inclination surely results from the fall, but one sins only if one begins to nurture the inclination by dwelling on how one might act on the attraction. In a similar way, a same-sex (or polygamous or pederastic) orientation is a result of the fall, but one does not sin (in the form of lust) unless one begins to dwell on and nurture that attraction in one's mind. Jesus's teaching on lust does not in any way make the distinction between same-sex orientation and same-sex practice problematic.

Argument 7: It Is Time for a Paradigm Shift

David Gushee, a good friend and prominent evangelical social ethicist, believes a paradigm shift is warranted—a paradigm shift that would fully affirm same-sex activity on the part of a gay Christian couple committed to an exclusive, lifelong, covenantal relationship.[48] He argues that personal experience with gay Christians, modern knowledge about the apparently unchangeable gay orientation of some people, and new biblical and hermeneutical analysis taken together warrant his rejection of what he acknowledges is the two-millennia-long teaching of the Christian church.

How should we evaluate this call for a paradigm shift? It is certainly the case that significant paradigm shifts have occurred in the history of the church. The Copernican revolution provides one excellent example. When Copernicus argued that the scientific data showed that the earth revolved around the sun rather than the sun circling the earth, prominent Christians like Martin Luther rejected Copernicus's ideas, citing biblical texts that say the sun stands still. And the Catholic Church forced Galileo to recant when he supported Copernicus with additional scientific data. But over time, virtually all Christians have embraced Copernicus's scientifically accurate view of the solar system. We now agree that the Bible is not intending to teach astronomy when it includes an occasional text that reflects a prescientific view of the earth and sun. Modern science has prompted a reassessment of exegetical and hermeneutical conclusions, and the result has been a paradigm shift.

Is Gushee's paradigm shift on gay sexual partnerships analogous to the paradigm shift on the solar system? Or is it more like the widespread embrace of divorce in the Christian community after the sexual revolution of the 1960s? In the latter case, societal values shifted quickly and dramatically (as they have more recently on same-sex relations), rejecting millennia-long Christian teaching on divorce. The response of the Christian church was to fall largely silent about Jesus's teaching against divorce and say little about the fact that Christians began to divorce at almost the same rate as everyone else. That paradigm shift, both Gushee and I agree, was a terrible ethical and theological mistake.

Finally, I simply do not find Gushee's arguments for his paradigm shift convincing. I respect the powerful personal experiences that he acknowledges played a role in his changed position. But personal experiences dare not override biblical teaching.

Gushee and others raise questions about the "traditional" interpretation of the relevant biblical texts. But I do not find the arguments compelling. And most advocates of a paradigm shift largely ignore the fact that the strongest biblical case for the view that God's design for sex is for a man and a woman committed to each other for life is the vast amount of biblical material that simply assumes that a male-female relationship is the proper place for sex. There is not a hint of any other situation being God's will. Even many pro-gay advocates acknowledge that the biblical material clearly supports the historic Christian position.

Nor do I find the hermeneutical arguments for this paradigm shift convincing. It is simply not true that the idea of a lifelong gay orientation is a totally modern idea unknown in the ancient Greco-Roman world. It is true that I would reject a number of the specific reasons given in Paul's time for opposing same-sex activity, but the Bible never cites these reasons in its general prohibition of gay sex. It is true that I embrace the paradigm shifts on both slavery and the role of women. But in both of those cases, there is a clear trajectory in the biblical canon that leads to that change. In the case of same-sex practice, there is not a hint of such a change in the Bible.

Obviously, we all are finite, limited persons. Our best ethical and theological judgments are filled with imperfection. We all see through a glass darkly. We cannot know now what the vast majority of Christians will think about this issue in one hundred years. All we can do is honestly and carefully affirm what we believe is the most faithful, biblical position. And I am convinced that the best biblical exegesis and hermeneutical reflection clearly points to the conclusion that the only right set-ting for sexual intercourse is between a man and a woman who are married and committed to an exclusive, lifelong relationship.

Thus far, I have argued that the biblical material unequivo-cally teaches that the only legitimate place for sexual intercourse is between a married man and woman in a lifelong committed relationship. Furthermore, none of the hermeneutical argu-ments claiming that Christians today should set aside the bibli-cal teaching are convincing. Now—much more briefly!—I turn to church history and then the global church today.

Why a discussion of these two areas? Because Christians over the ages have often rightly insisted that biblical interpretation and ethical and theological discussion should always occur in the whole body of Christ—both geographically and historically. One of the important protections against misguided biblical interpretation and theological reflection is to test one's conclu-sions with the full body of believers.

Church History

Does Christian history present a totally unanimous practice against same-sex sexual activity? Not quite. John Boswell's *Christianity, Social Tolerance and Homosexuality* (1980) shows that gay and lesbian sexual intimacy sometimes occurred in the history of the church.[49] But his claim that same-sex practice was not significantly condemned for the first one thousand years of church history is greatly overstated.[50]

A number of Christian writers in the first four centuries condemned same-sex intercourse—as did a church synod in AD 305–306. The church's teaching influenced Christian Roman emperors to increase the legal penalties for same-sex offenses. In the Middle Ages, church penitentials (which specified the

penance required for various sins) and official church pro-
nouncements (e.g., councils in 1179, 1212, and 1214) all condemned same-sex intimacy. And in the Reformation, the Protestant Reformers expressed the same position whenever they
mentioned the topic.

Stanley Grenz summarizes the historical record this way:

> Whenever the church was confronted with sexual practices
> involving persons of the same sex, Christian teachers spoke
> out against such behaviors. Despite differences among them,
> the ecclesiastical sources Boswell and others cite never express
> moral approval of, or even indifference to, same-sex activity. On
> the contrary, explicit moral references to such behavior in the
> Christian tradition were consistently negative. This suggests that
> Christian ethicists from the second century to the twentieth forge
> an unbroken chain. . . . In each era, Christian moralists rejected
> the same-sex practices of their day. And they consistently found
> the basis for such condemnation in the several scriptural texts in
> which the biblical authors appear to pronounce divine judgment
> on the homosexual behavior with which they were confronted.[51]

The Global Church Today

One-half of today's 2.2 billion Christians are Roman Catholics.
And the Catholic Church's teaching is unequivocal. Same-sex
acts are contrary to Scripture and natural law. In the words of the
Catechism: "Under no circumstances can they be approved."[52]
The Catechism also strongly urges respect, compassion, and
sensitivity to the men and women who have "deep-seated homosexual tendencies" but calls them to celibacy.[53]

The various Orthodox bodies contain 260 million Christians
(about 12 percent of all Christians today). Their teaching is similar to that of Roman Catholics. Orthodox writers, canons, and

synods from the earliest centuries to the present unanimously teach that "homosexual behavior is a sin."[54]

The vast majority (about 600 million) of today's Protestants (more than 800 million total) are evangelicals.[55] Not without exception but overwhelmingly, evangelicals today also embrace the historical teaching of the church on same-sex intercourse.

The explicit teaching of the churches that contain the vast majority of Christians today clearly declares that the only legitimate setting for sexual intercourse is within the marriage of a man and a woman. That is not to say that all these Christians embrace every argument advanced by the others for this conclusion.[56] Nor is it to ignore the fact that a significant minority of Christians in Western Europe and North America now affirm same-sex practice in lifelong covenanted partnerships.[57] But at the very least, the fact that the vast majority of Christians today embrace the historical teaching of the church as the proper interpretation of the Bible should give us pause before accepting same-sex intercourse.

It is also significant for Western evangelical Christians that the large majority of evangelicals today reside in the Global South—and they overwhelmingly believe that same-sex practice is contrary to God's will. If we want to escape a Western colonial mind-set, we must listen carefully to them. Young Christians today are well ahead of my generation in overcoming the condescending, even racist, attitudes of many white European and North American Christians. But transcending that white prejudice requires careful listening and dialoguing with the vast majority of evangelicals in the Global South who believe same-sex practice is not God's will. (One of the more striking recent examples of white "Western" arrogance is the way the relatively small number of Anglican/Episcopal churches in the West have refused to submit to the views of the vast majority of Anglicans worldwide who live in the Global South.) It is also striking that the embrace of the church's historic prohibition against same-sex practice is strongest in those parts of the world where the church is rapidly growing (the Global South) and weakest in those places where the church is declining (Western Europe, Canada, etc.). And in the United States, it is precisely those mainline denominations that are embracing same-sex relationships that have declined dramatically in the last forty-plus years while evangelical churches have done much better.

Listening to and dialoguing with other Christians, of course, does not mean simply accepting their viewpoints. Respectful dialogue in the global body of Christ includes challenging one another. I disagree, for example, with the laws (often supported by African evangelicals) in many African countries that pre-scribe the death penalty or prison for same-sex activity—and I have added my name to a letter from American evangelicals urging a different public policy. Dialogue in the global body of Christ must be a two-way street. Small minorities are sometimes right over against the vast majority.

At the very least, however, the fact that the teaching of the churches containing the overwhelming majority of contemporary Christians prohibits same-sex practice should be a significant factor in our thinking about this topic. And for evangelical Protestants, the fact that the vast majority of our evangelical sisters and brothers in the world today do the same should discourage us from quickly reversing the millennia-long teaching of the church.

A Better Approach

Simply repeating biblical truth (no matter how strong our exegesis or how sound our theology), listening to two millennia of church history, and dialoguing carefully with Christians in the Global South, however, are not enough. We need a substantially new approach.

For starters, we must do whatever it takes to nurture a generation of Christian men and women who keep their marriage vows and model healthy family life. By far the primary reason marriage is in such disarray in the West is that (Christian!) *heterosexuals* have not kept their marriage vows. If we want to restore marriage as a crucial foundation of a good culture, then our most important concern must be to persuade Christian heterosexuals to follow biblical norms.

Second, we need to find ways to love and listen to gay people, especially gay Christians, in a way that most of us have not done. (Andrew Marin's *Love Is an Orientation* issues a passionate summons to do that.)

In addition to living faithful marriages and engaging in loving conversation, I believe evangelicals must take the lead in a cluster of other activities related to gay people.

We ought to take the lead in condemning and combating verbal or physical abuse of gay people.

We need much better teaching on how evangelical parents should respond if their children announce that they are gay. Christian families should *never* reject a child, throw her out of their home, or refuse to see him if a child announces that he is gay. One can and should disapprove of unbiblical behavior without refusing to love and cherish a child who does that. Christian families should be the most loving places for children—even when they disagree with and act contrary to what parents believe. Please God, may we never hear another story of evangelical parents rejecting children who "come out of the closet."

We ought to develop model programs so that evangelical congregations are known as the best place in the world for gay and questioning youth (and adults) to seek God's will in a context that embraces, loves, and listens rather than shames, denounces, and excludes. Evangelical youth groups in our churches and organizations ought to be the safest place in the world for those wrestling with their sexual identity to be open about their struggle. Surely we can ask the Holy Spirit to show us how to teach and nurture biblical sexual practice without ignoring, marginalizing, and driving away from Christ those who struggle with biblical norms.

Our churches should be widely known as places where people with a gay orientation can be open about their orientation and feel truly welcomed and embraced. Of course, Christians who engage in unbiblical sexual practices (whether heterosexual or gay Christians) should be discipled (and disciplined) by the church and not allowed to be leaders or members in good standing if they persist in their sin. (The same should be said for those who engage in unbiblical practices of any kind, including greed and racism.) However, Christians who openly acknowledge a gay orientation but commit themselves to celibacy should be eligible for any role in the church that their spiritual gifts suggest. Imagine the impact if evangelical churches were widely known to be the best place in the world to find love, support, and full affirmation of gifts if one is an openly, unashamedly gay, celibate Christian.

That, very briefly, is what I believe our Lord calls biblical Christians to do on this fiercely debated, highly controversial topic.[58]

I have no illusions that this approach will be easy.

The secular media and many in our great universities are overwhelmingly opposed to the teaching of historic Christianity on sexuality.[59] In light of the Supreme Court's decision making same-sex marriage legal everywhere in the United States, there will be enormous legal and other public policy initiatives that will make it difficult for Christian nonprofits (universities, social service agencies, etc.) to maintain and live out the historic Christian teaching on same-sex activity.[60]

Many conservative Christians want only to condemn. Many gay people consider anything short of affirming same-sex intercourse to be intolerant and hateful. For some, "welcoming but not affirming" is unacceptable. For many in our relativistic society (where relativism is confused with tolerance, and "love" trumps truth), any statement, no matter how gentle and loving, that says certain behavior is sinful is rejected as intolerant, uncivil, hateful, and violent. We must beg the Holy Spirit to teach us better ways to be gentle and loving. But we also must realize that any condemnation of sin will sometimes be rejected as unloving by those who embrace sin.[61]

We dare not be misled by the theologically confused argument that since we are all sinners (which is certainly true), the church cannot say same-sex practice is sin. Just because every Christian fails God in some ways does not mean we should abandon biblical norms and stop speaking about sin. Rather, we should reaffirm God's standards and gently, patiently walk with each other to help us all become more and more conformed to the image of Christ.

Some Christians who have rightly learned to listen to and love gay people say that all we should do is love gay people— and then let the Holy Spirit teach each gay person how they should act. That is far too individualistic. The church through the centuries has believed that interpreting the Bible and nurturing biblical behavior is a communal task. We are supposed to watch over one another in love, as John Wesley said. The Christian community must discern how to understand biblical sexual teaching and then nurture Christians who live it—but always with love and gentleness.

And also patience. We are sometimes in too big of a hurry to summon people to live biblical ethics. All of us, if we look inward with honest hearts, recognize that the Holy Spirit has been very patient, slowly reshaping our tangled character into the image of Christ. We should not be in too big of a hurry to talk about biblical norms. We should love, pray, and listen, waiting patiently for the Holy Spirit to prompt us about when to speak and act.

But that does not mean never talking about biblical sexual standards. It means waiting for the Spirit's timing.

I hope and pray that the Lord of the church and the world will somehow weave love, truth, and fidelity out of the tangled strands that we currently face today on this issue. And I dare to hope that young evangelicals (like my coauthor of this book) will be wise and faithful leaders in that huge task.

❯ Response by Ben Lowe

Changing perspectives on human sexuality are causing upheaval in our churches and communities. They're among the most personal, painful, and polarizing moral questions stirring my generation today. And, regardless of what one believes, or how thoughtfully one approaches these issues, or how graciously one interacts with others, there's really no simple or safe way forward.

With a heavy heart, I mourn the hurt, fear, and anger that often plague these divisive issues and drive wedges between our families, friends, and fellow followers of Christ. At the same time, however, I'm glad things have become this challenging and unavoidable.

It's Good That It's Hard

For too long the church has largely been able to write off homosexuality as an outside problem. This contributed—through sins of commission as well as omission—to the tremendous insensitivity, misunderstanding, oppression, and even cruelty that persons identifying as, or suspected of being, LGBTQ have experienced. Today, however, just about everyone knows of loved ones who experience same-sex attraction and/or gender dysphoria.[62]

Being in relationship with those struggling with their sexuality or identifying as LGBTQ changes things dramatically for the heterosexual majority. Media and entertainment play a significant role here as well. All of a sudden this isn't an abstract, us-versus-them issue. It has become very personal. It is now *our* issue. Regardless of where things go from here, this more personal connection and understanding is a very significant step forward. And it's progress that can be celebrated no matter what each of us personally believes about these issues. It puts us on the path toward overcoming the ignorance and bigotry that have too often reigned, and the tragic damage and oppression that have resulted.

At the same time, this growing awareness of and connection to homosexuality, which is leading to its growing acceptance and helping to fuel the cultural shifts we're witnessing, is also giving rise to a backlash against those who hold what are now increasingly countercultural views. More situations are coming to light where Christians in particular are being criticized or even maligned for not affirming same-sex relationships. At least some of these cases are misguided and troubling.

How I long for all of us, regardless of sexual orientation, to see and treat one another as God sees and treats us! Until then, however, I'd rather have it be this way—where Christians may risk being discriminated against for maintaining unpopular

convictions—than the other way around where we're the aggres-
sors. Too often it's been LGBTQ persons—both Christian and
non-Christian—who have had to put up with injustice at the
church's hands. And that is truly tragic.

Samuel's Testimony

I'm grateful for the robust biblical and historical analysis that
my coauthor has offered in this chapter. In thinking through how
to respond, I corresponded with Samuel (not his real name), a
longtime friend of mine who is in his thirties, and who struggles
with same-sex attraction and has chosen a path of celibacy as
Ron advocates for here. This path has not been easy, so I'm
grateful that he was willing to share some of his experiences
and reflections for inclusion in this book.

I realize that some will be disappointed with aspects of Samuel's testimony or with my choice to feature it. I also recognize that
there are many stories from varying perspectives that should be
considered as we think through these issues. That said, Samuel's
journey has greatly influenced me, and I hope that, by sharing
part of his story here, others may benefit in some way too.

> I've struggled with same-sex attraction since I was a young boy,
> though I didn't understand it until later during my teenage years.
> It was terrifying to finally connect my feelings with homosexual-
> ity. "Gay" was a slur that my friends used to make fun of or insult
> others. They referred to homosexuals as "disgusting perverts."
> And here I was experiencing these unwanted attractions that
> wouldn't go away no matter how hard I tried. And I tried hard.
>
> I was terrified of somehow being found out, of not having close
> male friends because they would always be uneasy around me,
> of being judged and excluded from ministry by those at church,
> and of being alone later in life and unable to experience love or

lifelong intimacy with another person. It hurt so much not to be "normal," but I learned to mask my struggle and vowed to keep this hidden. On multiple occasions I absurdly imagined myself one day lying dead in a grave, relieved and satisfied that I had made it through life without anyone knowing my "dirty little secret."

A lot has happened since then. The secret eventually became too much to bear alone, and one day I broke down and tearfully opened up to my Christian parents. They instantly responded with love and comfort, and have continued to do everything they can to support me. Over the years, I've also confided in a select handful of mentors and friends. For me this is a very private issue, however, and not how I want to be known. Sure, it's a big part of my identity. But it does not ultimately define me. Christ does. He is my creator, provider, and redeemer. I'm learning to trust him, even when there's much that I don't understand.

Following Jesus means giving up everything but gaining immeasurably more in return. As Jesus taught, to be his disciples means denying ourselves, taking up our cross, and following him. For if we're all about saving our life then we will lose it, but if we lose our life for Christ and the gospel, then we will ultimately save it (see Mark 8:34b–35).

Sexuality is something that cuts to our core. Like everything else, however, it too has been affected by sin—in many ways, not just through same-sex attraction. And it too must be laid in love at the foot of the cross, to the one who sacrificed everything in order to save us. My broken sexuality is but one of the many effects of the fall, and neither it nor any other part of me falls beyond the redemptive love of God that is available in Christ Jesus. My best understanding of the Bible is that homosexual practice goes against God's will for us. As hard as this can be at times, I would rather surrender my homosexuality in worship to God and risk being mistaken than refuse to give it up and thus let it become an idol.

Celibacy is not always properly valued in parts of the church today, but it's certainly nothing new. Sure, unlike a heterosexual person who senses a call to celibacy, I'm sort of pushed into it without as much choice. But at the same time I *am* choosing to follow Jesus. That is my choice. And he's worth giving everything up for, like in the parables of the hidden treasure and the pearl (Matt. 13:44–46). As Christian writer A. W. Tozer puts it: "The man who has God for his treasure has all things in One. Many ordinary treasures may be denied him, or if he is allowed to have them, the enjoyment of them will be so tempered that they will never be necessary to his happiness. Or if he must see them go, one after one, he will scarcely feel a sense of loss, for having the Source of all things he has in One all satisfaction, all pleasure, all delight."[63]

Paths Forward

In figuring out the way forward, and regardless of our views, we need to take seriously both the thoughtful witness of Christians who affirm and embrace LGBTQ lifestyles as well as the witness of those who choose not to. At times it will take all the charity and patience God gives us in order to do this well. At other times we'll fall short, and then may God give us the humility and wisdom to seek help and forgiveness.

For those sincerely seeking clarity on these issues, it's one thing to conclude that homosexual practice is not biblically justified. It's another thing, however, to then live out this belief well in community. And this isn't just something for my generation to try to do better than previous ones. All generations need to work together to get this right. Two critical questions jump out here.

First, how do we tangibly and unreservedly love those who experience same-sex attraction? This includes figuring out what alternatives we can offer and how we can better support individuals struggling with their orientation or pursuing a life of celibacy. If someone chooses celibacy, there have to be more options available than a life of increasing loneliness and isolation (which is too often all that seems to be left).

There's often a strong and unbiblical bias in the church toward honoring marriage and families above singleness. Some churches will even only hire pastors and appoint elders who are married and have families. And when age cohorts reach the life stage where they pair off and get married, those who remain single are often left out, as couples tend to hang out with couples and families get together with other families that have kids around the same age. The church can and should be better than this. Couples can intentionally remember and value their single friends and relatives (regardless of sexual orientation). For instance, I know families that have made serious relational commitments to celibate individuals and have even welcomed them in as members of their household for the long term.

Along these lines, and in a society obsessed with sex, what does it look like to distinguish between sexual intimacy and other forms of healthy intimacy? Those committed to celibacy should not de facto be giving up on all forms of relational intimacy and devoted community. They should be empowered to cultivate loving, lifelong friendships and even be open to the possibility of nonromantic/nonsexual companionship as God provides. If two or more female friends or male friends end up single and choose to live celibate lives together over the longer term, that should be affirmed and not treated as odd or questionable.

The second critical question is, how do we tangibly and unreservedly love those who pursue sexual same-sex relationships if it runs counter to our values? This has challenging implications for Christian community, and I bring up some of these questions in my chapter on unity and reconciling our divisions. Beyond that, however, one step we can and should take is to distinguish between the expectations that we hold one another to within the bonds of Christian fellowship and the expectations that we hold others to in the broader society. For instance, I believe it is possible to support LGBTQ civil rights and same-sex civil marriage in society while also advocating for the right of churches to define sexual ethics and Christian marriage based on our religious beliefs. We should be wary about imposing distinctly Christian values or standards on others who don't share our faith, just as we don't want Islamic Sharia law imposed on non-Muslims like ourselves.

Living in the Tension

Recently I had a hard conversation with a good friend who is openly gay. He used to be a Christian but, after years of fighting his sexual orientation and asking God to change him, he decided to leave the faith to embrace homosexual relationships. While others may disagree with his assessment, he just couldn't see a biblical way to do both at the same time.

We remained in contact through all this, and one day he asked to talk about something that had been weighing on him for some time. He knows my thoughts on sexual ethics and wanted to know whether I would be disappointed if his behavior never changed. I responded that I would be overjoyed if he returned to faith and rejoined me as a brother in Christ. Regardless of his faith commitment or sexual behavior, however, I still cared about him and wanted to remain friends. In the end, we agreed that, while each of us experiences tensions at times because of our differences, our friendship is more important and worth the tension. It wasn't an easy conversation, but I'm grateful for his graciousness toward me, and glad that our friendship continues.

I don't have all the answers here. I don't think any of us do. And the stakes sure are high. But I hope and pray that as we live into the tensions of the present, God will help us find ways—without minimizing our beliefs and values—to love one another well here, and that Christians will more and more become known as a just, peaceful, and caring people toward the LGBTQ community and all those who experience same-sex attraction.

DISCUSSION QUESTIONS

1. Ron says: "Jesus never condoned sin. But he modeled amazing love and concern for those ensnared by its destructive power." To what extent does your church follow Jesus's example with regard to sinners in general and sexual sinners in particular?

2. "By far the primary reason marriage is in such disarray in the West is that (Christian!) *heterosexuals* have not kept their marriage vows," writes Ron. If it's true that the primary threat to marriage in the West is coming from Christian heterosexuals, what should be your church's agenda going forward from here?

3. How has your church taken "the lead in condemning and combating verbal or physical abuse of gay people"? How could it do more?

4. What do you think about Ron's statement that "Christians who openly acknowledge a gay orientation but commit themselves to celibacy should be eligible for any role in the church that their spiritual gifts suggest"?

5. Ben calls for the church to figure out "what alternatives we can offer and how we can better support individuals

struggling with their orientation or pursuing a life of celibacy. If someone chooses celibacy, there have to be more options available than a life of increasing loneliness and isolation." What are some of the alternatives your church currently provides or could potentially provide?

PART 2

Ben Lowe's Chapters

(with Ron Sider's Responses)

6

Will We Live More Like Jesus?

BEN LOWE

> The greatest single cause of atheism in the world today is Christians who acknowledge Jesus with their lips and walk out the door and deny him by their lifestyle. This is what an unbelieving world simply finds unbelievable.[1]

A recording of this quote spoken by Brennan Manning was featured at the beginning of the DC Talk song "What If I Stumble?," which was popular during my childhood in the 1990s. It continues to resonate with my generation today as we struggle to reconcile what the Bible teaches us with what many of us Christians actually look like.

So my first question for older generations—and this forms the foundation for my other three questions (chapters) as well—has to do with the core issue of discipleship: "Why doesn't the church look more like the Jesus we claim to follow?"

My parents' and grandparents' generations have placed a strong emphasis on holding the right beliefs. Truth is important, and ever more so when it impacts our eternal destiny. So our churches and denominations work hard to define and safeguard orthodoxy—what we should believe. But what's the point of believing the right things if we don't then live them out?

Orthodoxy should lead to orthopraxy—right belief should lead to right living. But too often it doesn't, and this is where the disconnect and disillusionment come in. Of course, it's hard to ask a question like this without seeming (or actually being) hypocritical. None of us measures up to Christ, and it seems foolish to be comparing ourselves to one another to see who comes closer. We're admittedly all implicated in some way here.

I'm not referring to fringe groups like Westboro Baptist Church, the small Kansas congregation infamous for preaching hate and picketing the funerals of slain soldiers. Few are under the illusion that groups like this represent the gospel or church in any real way.

But what about *our* churches? What about *us*? We're taught that Christians are being transformed in distinct and meaningful ways, that we're "in the world but not of it." But then why do we so often look more like the surrounding culture than like Jesus? Why do Christian marriages seem to fall apart at the same rate as non-Christian marriages? Why do we spend so much money on bigger and more lavish homes or church building projects while many in our communities remain hungry or homeless? Why do we entertain sins like gossip and materialism, and why do we measure the success of a church by the size of its congregation? Why are Christians known more for being judgmental and self-righteous than loving and humble?

In 2014, horrific news reports came out of the Central African Republic about so-called Christian gangs that were indiscriminately murdering their Muslim neighbors on a large scale, in revenge for similar Muslim violence toward Christians stemming from a 2013 military coup. The situation quickly spiraled out of control, and thousands of Muslims—the vast majority of whom were innocent of the earlier violence—fled for their lives. While Christians have long been victims of persecution, this is yet another tragic instance where people *claiming* the name of Christ became the perpetrators of terror and suffering instead. How can followers of Christ be responsible for such evil when the second-greatest commandment is to love our neighbors as ourselves, and when Jesus commands us to love even our enemies?

We also see various forms of Christian-perpetrated injustice alive and well all around us in the United States. Some of my friends and I recently found out that the owner of one of our favorite local restaurants confiscates the tips from his servers and rebukes them when they don't collect enough during their shift. Needless to say, we don't eat there anymore, and we discourage others from going too. The saddest part is that the owner is a regular churchgoer, he plays Christian music in the restaurant, and his employees all know that he identifies as a Christian. But then why doesn't his faith compel him to treat them with greater justice and charity?

I served as a youth group counselor at my church for a number of years. Throughout that time, I noticed an inconsistency with the priorities that some—though not all—of our parents have for their children. They bring their kids to church so that they grow into "good Christians" who stay out of trouble (no drugs, alcohol, premarital sex, etc.) and are polite and obedient. Tensions can arise in some families, however, if their kids grow "too passionate" about their faith and begin investing too much time in church. Or, even worse, if they begin exploring vocational ministry and missions! There's significant social pressure to go to a prestigious college, get a high-paying job, and live a materially well-off life. Why are such worldly goals often emphasized at the cost of biblical priorities? Perhaps this phenomenon varies from culture to culture, but I've certainly experienced and observed it quite prominently in the Chinese American churches I've belonged to.

Whatever the specific illustration—and there are many to choose from—it's troubling that much of the American church seems to be Christian in name only. We often don't reflect the life and teachings of Christ very much.

The gospel doesn't just save; it also transforms. At least it's supposed to. "Therefore, if anyone is in Christ, [they are] a new creation. The old has passed away; behold, the new has come" (2 Cor. 5:17 ESV). The apostle Paul emphasizes this theme repeatedly throughout his letters: "You were taught, with regard to your former way of life, to put off your old self, which is being corrupted by its deceitful desires; to be made new in the attitude of your minds; and to put on the new self, created to be like God in true righteousness and holiness. . . . Follow God's example, therefore, as dearly loved children" (Eph. 4:22–24; 5:1).

Granted, we may never be completely free from sin and brokenness in this life, but we are actively in the process of being sanctified. And Jesus taught that we can tell a tree by its fruit (see Matt. 12:33; Luke 6:44). There should be signs of growth and transformation in every area of our lives and churches.

So why is this so often and so deeply lacking? Where is the fruit?

The more I struggle with this, however, the more it seems to break down into two interconnected questions, one having to do with our worldview and the other having to do with our lifestyle.

Worldview: Is the Faith That Many of Us Were Raised in More Cultural Than Biblical?

In other words, why is there so much cultural accommodation and compromise in our churches? Rev. Peter Harris, cofounder of the international Christian conservation organization A Rocha, put it this way in a chapel message at Wheaton College:

Lots of people are worried about genetically modified foods, but Christians should be concerned about whether we belong to a "genetically modified church." I wonder if the DNA of our deeply materialistic, narcissistic, and individualistic culture has become so patched into our reading of what it means to be a Christian that we are not talking the biblical gospel any longer.[2]

I resonate with what Peter is describing here. As a pastor's kid—and a missionary's kid before that—I've been immersed in the church my whole life. And there are many things I've experienced or witnessed in churches that trouble me deeply and seem more closely aligned with our culture than with the Bible. Here are some examples:

- pastors and leaders who act like celebrities and who are heavily self-promotional
- performance-driven services that turn congregations into audiences and worship into entertainment—smoke machines and mood lighting included
- popular "feel-good" or "self-help" sermons that are light on the gospel and have little actual teaching from Scripture
- worship songs that are largely focused on the individual, with lyrics that emphasize "I/me," even though we sing them together in groups and congregations
- patriotic worship songs, sung especially around the Fourth of July, that confuse Christianity with nationalism
- conspicuously extravagant church buildings and lifestyles of unrestrained consumption that are celebrated instead of being questioned
- regular church hopping from popular church to popular church in an often never-ending search for a satisfying worship experience that best "fits" the "consumer"
- support for unjust wars, state-sponsored violence, and even torture in the name of our national interest or security

- the dominance of fear over love as the motivating factor in engaging the world; fear of Muslims, LGBTQ people, immigrants, socialists, environmentalists, the poor, and so on

Christianity has enjoyed a privileged position in the United States since the country was founded. Being an entrenched part of the status quo, it's easy and comfortable to identify as Christian in America. But I wonder if we have allowed that comfort to insulate us, and in turn we have become complacent. Instead of renewing society in redemptive ways, have we allowed the culture to infect and dilute our faith? At the end of the day, are we following the God of the Bible or some other god that we've cobbled together in the likeness of ourselves and our culture? "Do not conform to the pattern of this world, but be transformed by the renewing of your mind. Then you will be able to test and approve what God's will is—his good, pleasing, and perfect will" (Rom. 12:2).

Jason Fileta

Director of Micah Challenge USA

When I was in high school I made a decision—that if it was possible to follow Jesus and say nothing about injustice in the world, then I wanted nothing to do with him.

I should provide some more context for you. My parents immigrated here from Egypt, and I grew deeply aware of and disturbed by persecution, poverty, discrimination, and other injustices faced by my family around the world. Not only was my heart broken over injustice, but I knew that God's heart was as well. I was taught that God did not intend the world to be this way and that the deepest grief over injustice in our world wasn't mine to bear but God's. However, in my Christian school I learned something different.

In high school I was surrounded by a "Christian" culture that believed it was entirely possible to be a disciple and say nothing about the persecution of my family in Egypt. On a grander scale, in my community of faith, *it was possible to be a disciple and do nothing about injustice.* In fact, if I did everything I was taught, I would grow up to be a pious, wealthy, and completely unconcerned global citizen. *This vision of discipleship spoiled my appetite for faith.*

It wasn't until I read the Bible for the first time that I discovered I had rejected a counterfeit Jesus! Jesus of Nazareth not only lived a life filled with compassion for the poor and marginalized, but he commanded his disciples to do the same. In fact, it became clear to me that there was no way to follow Jesus and *not* say something about injustice—with words and deeds. My faith was restored, and I've been flying by the seat of my pants ever since.

I grieve for my friends who too have rejected Christ but not yet discovered that the Jesus they rejected is simply a counterfeit that largely lives inside the suburbs of the American church. May we rediscover the true Jesus—filled with compassion, focused on restoration of body and soul, and unable to ignore injustice.

Lifestyle: Have We Become Compartmentalized Christians Who Go to Church on Sunday but Don't Let the Gospel Completely Transform Our Lives?

In other words, why is there often such a gap between what we claim to believe and how we actually live?

Many of us go to church, wear nice clothes, smile, and act the part, but then live the rest of our lives relatively indistinguishably from the world in a lot of ways. Some of us sing worship songs about surrendering all to Jesus but hoard our resources and organize our lives around selfish goals and personal dreams. Others of us are respectable Christians on Sunday but shamelessly mistreat our employees or family during the rest of the week (as I noted about the owner of my former favorite restaurant). Yet others among us take aggressive stances against sexual sin in public but in private are pursuing some form of sexual immorality or addiction. And some of us quote chapters like Romans 1 and 2 Corinthians 12 to judge people who are homosexual but then engage uncritically in gossip, arrogance, disobedience, selfish ambition, fits of rage, and more, all of which are warned against in those very same passages.

Where is the authenticity and the holistic, lifelong, and radical discipleship that Jesus taught and modeled? Or can we fairly be compared to the Pharisees and religious leaders whom Jesus railed against and called white-washed tombs—looking good on the outside but filled with rotting flesh and dry bones on the inside? "Be on your guard against the yeast of the Pharisees, which is hypocrisy," Jesus warns. "There is nothing concealed that will not be disclosed, or hidden that will not be made known" (Luke 12:1b–2).

Dietrich Bonhoeffer, the German pastor and theologian killed by the Nazis, described this as cheap versus costly grace in his seminal book, *The Cost of Discipleship*. On one hand, cheap grace is "the preaching of forgiveness without requiring repentance, baptism without church discipline, Communion without confession, absolution without personal confession. Cheap grace is grace without discipleship, grace without the cross, grace without Jesus Christ, living and incarnate."[3]

But, on the other hand, cheap grace is really not grace at all. It's a sham. True grace is costly: "It is costly because it costs a [person his] life, and it is grace because it gives a [person] the only true life. It is costly because it condemns sin, and grace because it justifies the sinner. Above all, it is costly because it cost God the life of his Son: 'ye were bought at a price,' and what has cost God much cannot be cheap for us."[4]

Jesus gave up everything for us and calls us to take up our cross and follow him. There is no halfway, lukewarm, or compartmentalized response to the gospel. The apostles, Saint Francis of Assisi, William Wilberforce, Hudson Taylor, Dietrich Bonhoeffer, Oscar Romero, Mother Teresa, and many other heroes of the faith were all very different people with unique callings, but they had one thing in common: their visible and radical devotion to Christ. Why aren't we more like them?

Exceptions versus the Norm

To be fair, for every negative example I've mentioned in this chapter, whether it has to do with our worldview or our lifestyle, I can also think of positive exceptions.

I can think of Christians who are living with integrity, who work hard to understand and apply biblical values throughout their lives, who are appropriately upfront about their struggles, and who show grace to those around them. I can think of Christians who love their enemies, serve their neighbors sacrificially, and pursue Christ with abandon. But these shouldn't be the exceptions; they should be the norm.

Living a neutered faith doesn't impact just us. It also affects our witness to the world. This isn't a new problem—the apostle Paul had strong words for his fellow Jews who didn't practice what they preached: "As it is written, God's name is blasphemed among the Gentiles because of you" (Rom. 2:24)—but it's no less troubling and problematic. In a world inundated with many competing claims, actions speak louder than words, and our lives either authenticate or detract from the witness of the gospel.

So how can we work together with the Holy Spirit and across generations to transform the church into a body that is defined more by Jesus than by our surrounding culture and that is completely devoted to him with our whole lives?

Response by Ron Sider

This chapter makes me want to weep. As young evangelicals look at my generation, they see vast numbers of Christians—vast numbers of self-proclaimed evangelicals!—whose lives look almost the same as their unbelieving neighbors. And the hypocrisy turns people away from the Lord Jesus I adore.

I have sometimes said in more recent years that I have largely resolved the intellectual doubts that I wrestled with in university. But one substantial reason for doubting the truth of Christianity remains: the church. When the New Testament promises that in the power of the Risen Lord and with the Holy Spirit dwelling within us, Christians can refuse to be conformed to this world and truly live like Jesus; when the gospel promises that and then Christians live like the world, one has to ask whether the gospel is really true after all.

Ben is absolutely right. The same reality that drives his hard questions impelled me to write *The Scandal of the Evangelical Conscience: Why Are Christians Living Just like the Rest of the World?*[5] If Christianity is to have integrity and flourish in the next few decades, we must figure out why so many in my generation have failed to live like Jesus. And even more important, we must discover ways to become more faithful.

Ben is quite right to expect that orthodoxy (right doctrine) should lead to orthopraxy (right practice). And he correctly notes that evangelicals have invested a lot of time in seeking to defend orthodoxy. But I think that one big part of the problem is that evangelical theology itself has not been nearly as orthodox as we have claimed. To cite just one example: there are hundreds of Bible verses that teach that God and God's faithful people have a special concern for the poor, but not one evangelical preacher in fifty in my generation preached as much about the poor as the Bible does. And that is by no means the only area where evangelicals have failed to be biblical.

In fact, I think that one major reason for the failure that Ben rightly laments is precisely that evangelical theology has failed to be biblical at many crucial points. Let me mention several: our definition of the gospel, salvation, sin, justice, and wealth.

Right at the center of the cheap grace that leads to Christians living like the world is the widespread evangelical tendency *to reduce the gospel* to forgiveness of sins. Many taught us that the primary (perhaps only) reason Jesus came was to die as the substitutionary atonement for our sins so we could go to heaven when we die. Some of our best theologians claimed that the central, primary Christian doctrine is justification by faith alone. The meaning of the gospel is the forgiveness of sins. But if the gospel is only the forgiveness of sins, then we can accept the gospel, receive God's forgiveness, be on our way to heaven— and then live like hell until we get there. We can receive God's forgiveness given through Jesus's cross and still go on living the same racist, adulterous, materialistic life as before.

In fact, however, reducing the gospel just to forgiveness of sins is profoundly unbiblical, indeed unorthodox and heretical. Jesus always defined the gospel as the good news of the kingdom (Mark 1:14–15; Luke 4:43).[6] He meant that the messianic kingdom long promised by the prophets was actually breaking into history in his person and work. Certainly forgiveness of sins was central to Jesus's gospel of the kingdom. The only way to enter Jesus's dawning kingdom was to accept God's amazing forgiveness. But the other half of Jesus's gospel of the kingdom was that the messianic time of peace, justice, and right relationships in every area of life was actually beginning to take visible, concrete shape. Jesus was not a lone ranger going around the country whispering to isolated hermits: "Your sins are forgiven." He gathered a circle of forgiven sinners into a new community that began to live out the teaching of Jesus's kingdom ethics. In Jesus's new kingdom community, Jesus's disciples must keep their marriage vows, the rich must share radically with the poor, women must be treated with full dignity, and we must love even our enemies. Jesus's gospel of the kingdom has both vertical and horizontal dimensions.

Next, the biblical understanding of *salvation* has been individualized and privatized by evangelicals in a way similar to what we did with the gospel. Salvation has been reduced to a personal affair between me and Jesus so I can be forgiven and go to heaven. Again, thank God that forgiveness of sins is central to what the New Testament teaches about salvation; I never want to stand before our holy God on any basis other than that Jesus atoned for my sins on the cross and enables me now to stand before God clothed with Christ's righteousness. But a quick look at the words for salvation in the New Testament shows that they include both "justification by faith" and "sanctification of sinners" so that day by day we become more like Christ. And salvation also includes the transformed relations in the body of Christ.

The story of Zacchaeus is striking. He was an unjust tax collector who became rich by taking advantage of a very unjust system. But when he met Jesus, he gave back all that he had taken wrongly and gave generously to poor people. There is not a word in the story about forgiveness of sins, although Jesus undoubtedly forgave the rascal. What the story emphasizes is the transformed economic relationships that happened after Zacchaeus met Jesus. The story ends with Jesus's words: "Today salvation has come to this house" (Luke 19:9). Again and again in the epistles, salvation words are used to refer to the transformed socioeconomic relations in the body of Christ (Rom. 14:17; Eph. 2:11–3:7).[7]

Evangelicals have also often preached a less-than-biblical understanding of *sin*. Very often, they have limited their understanding and preaching about sin to personal sins like lying, stealing, and sexual disobedience. But the Bible also condemns unjust socioeconomic structures like unfair legal systems and unjust economic systems.[8] When evangelicals see sin as only personal, then they can major on sexual sin and neglect economic and racial injustice. A biblically balanced understanding of sin as both personal and social helps us deal both with the tragic widespread sexual brokenness of our time and also the widespread racial and economic injustice.

At least as astounding is the way most evangelical preachers of my generation largely ignored the hundreds of Bible verses about God's concern for the poor. (When I collected all these verses in one place, the book was two hundred pages long![9]) The theme that God and his faithful people have a special concern for the poor is perhaps the second most common theme in the Bible.[10] Jesus even said that if we fail to feed the hungry and clothe the naked, we go to hell (Matt. 25:41–46). But for much of my lifetime, most evangelical preachers failed to even come close to talking about God's concern for the poor as often as the Bible does. How can we claim to be orthodox—and biblical—if we largely ignore one of the most central themes of the Bible?

Also unbiblical has been the evangelical treatment of *justice* in my lifetime. For starters, many evangelical preachers and teachers did not talk about justice at all—even though it is a frequent theme in the Bible. And when they did mention it, they often reduced justice to procedural justice—as long as the procedures (e.g., the legal processes) are fair, then the outcome is just even if some people are in poverty and others are very wealthy. But a careful examination of the biblical teaching on justice shows that God's understanding of justice includes not only procedural justice (i.e., fair courts) but also distributive justice (i.e., a fair distribution of the productive resources). God wants every family and person to have access to the productive resources (e.g., land or knowledge) so that if they work responsibly they can earn their own way and be dignified members of society.[11] If that is what the biblical teaching on justice means, then evangelical Christians must be deeply engaged in correcting unjust systems so that everyone has genuine opportunity.

Finally, not many evangelicals understand the full biblical teaching on *wealth*. The Bible does teach that a generous sufficiency of material possessions is a good gift from the Creator. The Bible also says that when we live the way the Creator intends, the result (other things being equal) is material blessing (Deut. 6:1–3; 28:2; Prov. 15:6). But some preachers teach a gospel of wealth (if we obey God, we will be rich) and ignore the many biblical texts that say that people often get rich by oppressing others and in that case God is angry with them (Ps. 10:2–18; Isa. 3:14–25; Jer. 5:26–29). Furthermore, the Bible frequently warns that riches are dangerous because they tempt us to forget God (Deut. 8:11–14, 17; Luke 18:24; 1 Tim. 6:9–10). Since so few of our preachers teach a biblically balanced understanding of wealth, justice, and the poor, it is not surprising that so many Christians embrace a materialistic lifestyle.

One major reason that so many evangelical Christians (and other Christians too!) live such unfaithful Christian lives is that our theology has not been nearly as biblical as we have claimed.

One part of the solution for the tragic failure that Ben rightly laments is better—more biblical, more orthodox—theology.

Ben rightly points to the way Christians often compartmentalize their lives as one cause of the problem. Too many Christians try to apply biblical standards on Sunday and in the home and then live by different norms at work. Sometimes they consciously or unconsciously have a sacred/secular dichotomy. The church and perhaps the home and family are part of the sacred realm where Jesus's norms apply. The secular world of work has different norms. But again, this confusion finally rests in bad theology. Biblical faith says Christ is Lord of all of life: boardroom and bedroom, family and work, church and politics. Compartmentalization and a sacred/secular dualism are finally bad theology.

It is probably helpful to see today's failure of Christians to follow Jesus as part of a perennial temptation. I think that one of the greatest failures of Christians over the two millennia of our history is the recurring pattern of slowly conforming to surrounding culture rather than living Jesus's kingdom way. Whether the temptation is materialism, sexual promiscuity, idolatrous nationalism, or whatever, the easy, comfortable path is to slowly accept the values and practices of surrounding society rather than choose the difficult path of challenging and defying accepted norms and practices. Every culture affirms some biblical norms and rejects many others. That means that Christians in every culture must be deeply countercultural.

The early Christians were quite clear on this point. Paul pleaded with the Roman church not to be conformed to this world (Rom. 12:2) and urged the Corinthian Christians to "come out from [non-Christians] and be separate" (2 Cor. 6:17). In 1 Peter, Christians are described as "aliens and exiles" (2:11 RSV). Stanley Hauerwas and William H. Willimon captured these biblical summons very effectively in their book *Resident Aliens*.[12]

But living out Jesus's radical kingdom norms in the midst of a fallen culture is always hard. It requires living in constant tension with what is wrong in the culture. Over the centuries, a few Christians have resolved this tension by withdrawing physically (e.g., the hermits and the Amish). Most Christians have reduced the tension by slowly conforming (and finding rationales to conform) to surrounding society's values. Both approaches are wrong. The Lord wants us to live in the midst of fallen culture and model a new, countercultural reality.

Fifty years ago, most evangelicals did see themselves as a countercultural community. But in the last several decades, evangelicals have largely lost that self-understanding. If Christians today are going to follow Jesus rather than today's culture (whether in the area of sexual practice, material possessions, marriage and divorce, nationalism, or abortion), we must recover a deep understanding of being a countercultural community. That does not mean returning to the specifics of evangelical countercultural practice in the 1950s (no dancing, alcohol, or movies). But deciding to follow Jesus today will mean countercultural lifestyles that refuse to conform to today's widespread materialism, idolatrous nationalism, and failure to respect the sanctity of every person.

Ben's final paragraph raises an enormously important question. Can we work together across the generations to transform the church so that it is defined by Jesus rather than today's culture? I devoutly hope so, but I certainly do not know in any detail how to do that.

But a few thoughts occur to me. This book is obviously one small attempt at listening and cooperating across the generations. (I'm old enough to be Ben's grandfather!) We need to be careful to have many congregations that bring together everyone from children to seniors. Major gatherings of Christian leaders could do much more to be sure all the generations have a substantial voice. That would probably mean that important gatherings of Christian leaders largely organized by younger Christians would carefully invite significant numbers of older leaders. The reverse would be important in events largely organized by more senior leaders.

Perhaps some group of Christians should decide to organize a new set of events and avenues of communication that would have as their primary focus a deeper, more extensive intergenerational dialogue among the Christian leaders. Might it not be helpful to have a regular national event (or several regional events) where there were equal numbers of Christian leaders under forty and over forty and the agenda was serious, substantial dialogue on the crucial issues facing the church today? A new or existing Christian publication could embrace the same agenda. Christian publishing houses could develop a series of books with a similar purpose.

In intergenerational dialogue, we could together assess what has so badly gone wrong in my generation. Together we could confess where we have failed and discern how to avoid those failures in the future. We could together listen anew to the Bible to discover a more faithful approach. And together we could plead with God to show us how to be more faithful to Christ our Lord.

I have no magic formula for accomplishing serious, sustained intergenerational dialogue. But I believe it is essential. Whether Christian leaders over forty like it or not, the crucial decisions about the shape of the church will increasingly be made by those who are under forty today. I hope it is not just because I am seventy-six years old that I think a far deeper intergenerational dialogue would bless us all.

Somehow, please God, may our church learn how, in the power of the Holy Spirit, to live the kind of common life that will attract others to Christ and please our Lord.

DISCUSSION QUESTIONS

1. Ben asks, "Is the faith that many of us were raised in more cultural than biblical?" What would be some of your own examples of a faith more cultural than biblical?

2. This chapter challenges us to consider whether we are confining God's influence in our lives to Sunday only. What are some of the recent ways that the gospel has been transforming your Monday through Saturday life?

3. Ron writes, "The only way to enter Jesus's dawning kingdom was to accept God's amazing forgiveness. But the other half of Jesus's gospel of the kingdom was that the messianic time of peace, justice, and right relationships in every area of life was actually beginning to take visible, concrete shape." Is your church a community where both halves of the gospel are emphasized?

4. It is common to hear Christians lament the worsening moral state of our country. Implicit seems to be the concept that this decline is caused by people outside the church abandoning biblical teachings on sexuality. How can we move our churches to lament our own participation in the immorality of abandoning biblical teaching on greed, possessiveness, indifference to the poor, favoritism toward the rich, injustice, destruction of God's creation, and destruction of marriage?

5. If you are an older leader in your church, what steps could you take to bring younger people into positions of leadership? If you did take those steps, how could you personally come alongside to help those younger people to succeed (instead of simply expecting them to succeed)? What sacrifices in your personal time would you be willing to make?

7

Will We Renew
Our Political Witness?

BEN LOWE

Immigration reform, desperately needed and long overdue, was finally supposed to happen back in 2013.

Advocates for reform had grown into a powerful political force made up of leaders and groups from across ideological divides—including the business community, religious community, unions, law enforcement, immigrants themselves, and many others—in what was the largest, loudest, and broadest political movement the United States had seen in years. Both Democrats and Republicans agreed that millions of people were being impacted every year by a broken and antiquated immigration system, and there was just too much momentum for things to stall this time.

Yet, remarkably, there would be no reform in 2013. The Senate passed a bipartisan bill by a strong 68–32 vote (though it should have been stronger!), and President Obama communicated that he would sign it into law. But House leadership pushed reform off in 2013, in the midst of unexpected political crises and Tea Party opposition, and refused to let it go to a vote in 2014.

How can an issue as urgent and broadly supported as this get held up so long and by so few? If we can't even pass immigration reform after years of bipartisan efforts, then what chance do we have of addressing the many other pressing challenges dragging the country down? Is there hope for the state of politics in the United States, which is seen as a beacon of democracy for the rest of the world?

Disillusioned and Disaffected

That many Americans are deeply disillusioned by politics should surprise no one. Congress regularly languishes with approval ratings in the single digits and, in a brilliant 2013 poll, was ranked worse than traffic jams, root canals, head lice, cockroaches, colonoscopies, used-car salesmen, and even Genghis Khan (Congress did, however, manage to beat out telemarketers, North Korea, Ebola, gonorrhea, and meth labs).[1]

People of all political persuasions agree that many of our societal systems—education, health care, immigration, criminal justice, national security, infrastructure, and so on—are broken and in desperate need of fixing. But perhaps one of the greatest challenges to progress on these urgent priorities is that our *political system* has become increasingly dysfunctional. The very process for fixing our problems is itself broken.

Even more troubling to many Christians in my generation, however, is the track record of Christian (and particularly evangelical) engagement in the political sphere. We're ashamed of how God and our faith have often been portrayed in the public square. The shrill, narrow, and hyperpartisan ideology of the culture-warring religious right that has dominated the evangelical public witness for more than a generation (along with, at times, the minority religious left) has proven largely ineffective and biblically truncated or inconsistent. During this time, Christian leaders in the public square have offered valuable (and often overlooked) contributions, but many have also caused considerable and persisting damage.

Such toxic baggage chases people away from the faith, and chases the faithful—especially those of us in the millennial generation—away from politics. Many younger Christians today consider themselves political orphans and are exchanging civic and political engagement for charitable and community service. This is especially problematic.

It's one thing to be dismayed by broken sociopolitical structures in the world. But if our Christian witness in the public square is often also a source of despair, then where do we turn? As the late evangelical church leader John Stott once said: "We should not ask, 'What is wrong with the world?' for that diagnosis has already been given. Rather, we should ask, 'What has happened to the salt and light?'"[2]

Longing for an Alternative

This isn't just an abstract discussion for me. It's also very personal. I grew up in a strong evangelical family that consistently voted Republican for generations. I came of age in a post-9/11 world, however, and my political views grew more nuanced as my understanding of both global affairs and biblical ethics deepened.

Since when were there only three main priorities for all Christians to care about—abortion, homosexuality, and religious freedom? Since when did being pro-life only narrowly mean being antiabortion, and not also antipoverty, antiwar, pro–health care, pro-environment, and more? Since when did it become okay to build political support by preying on people's fears and demonizing those considered different from ourselves?

Jenny Yang

Vice President of Advocacy and Policy, World Relief

We need to reengage the evangelical community to understand the importance of politics and advocacy, not just for a robust Christian witness but also to deepen our own personal discipleship. For too long, many Christians, young evangelicals in particular, have become disillusioned with politics because it's considered dirty, untruthful, or ineffective—and it has been all of those things. This shouldn't excuse us, however, from an opportunity to shape a better public narrative and to foster a politics that can work to help the most vulnerable of our society. At a time when a growing number of evangelicals care about social justice, we must be stewards of our influence to address the root causes of violence, conflict, poverty, and oppression—which often can happen only through political action—and do so with a spirit of humility, love, and patience. There is a difference between being political and being partisan. We should be political, engaging with our elected officials to ensure that the laws they pass and the policies they support reflect the values we hold dear. However, that should not lead us to partisanship, which is where we pledge blind allegiance to one political party over another. If evangelicals do not recapture a spirit of Christ-centered political engagement, we will leave a vacuum to be filled by others who don't speak for our values or priorities. Ultimately, we are called to advocate for others, just as Jesus is an advocate for all humanity, taking the sins of the world upon himself and interceding on our behalf before God (1 John 2:1).

Over time, I became disaffected by things that I used to take for granted as being right and good—American foreign policy, the Republican party, and the religious right in particular. I longed for prophetic alternatives that crossed traditional partisan boundaries, moved beyond religious stereotypes, and offered a renewed model of faithful politics defined by love and reconciliation instead of fear and division.

This longing grew so strong that when an unexpected opportunity arose to run for Congress, I surprised myself and just about everyone else by agreeing. Never having studied political science, voted in a primary election, or participated in a political party, I was a remarkably unlikely, inexperienced, and poorly connected candidate for elected office. And I was only twenty-five years old.

But I was also surrounded by Christian friends and colleagues who were, like me, sick of the status quo and eager to see something different—even if that meant trying to create an alternative ourselves. The likelihood of winning this election was slim (we ended up getting 37 percent of the vote), but that expectation freed us up to run a campaign where we weren't afraid of losing. We didn't have to compromise our principles or hold back in any way, and we didn't face the temptation to play negative or cut corners in order to win more votes. We could engage in politics based simply on what we thought was right and good, not what was expedient and popular. And so for a remarkable and challenging year, we strived to do just that.

What We Found

The campaign was one of the most trying things I've ever done, but I remain deeply grateful for the experience and encouraged by the fruit we witnessed. I've written more about it in another book—*Doing Good Without Giving Up*[3]—but there are two takeaways in particular that I'd like to share here.

First, we found that many fellow Christians today are very hesitant to get politically involved or even to vote. I was surprised that some of my friends withheld their support, not because they didn't agree with my positions or motives, but because they viewed politics in general and Christian politics in particular as beyond redemption. For them, politics has become such a broken system and corrupting culture that it's impossible to participate in it without eventually becoming corrupt as well. There are rich theological discussions to be had about the appropriate role of Christians in politics. But that wasn't what we usually ran up against here. What we encountered most often was cynicism.

However, the second lesson we learned is that cynicism doesn't have to win. Being involved in politics without compromising one's faith may not be easy, but it can be done. And it can also be surprisingly fruitful.

I ran as a pro-life Democrat—and we could have a long conversation about the pros and cons of running on the platform of either major party—and being open about my faith was often not pleasant. I took considerable flak from many (mostly Caucasian) evangelicals who were not used to seeing a Christian run as a Democrat, and I also took flak from many Democrats who are not used to having a pro-life evangelical as their candidate. Over time, however, our campaign was able to build bridges between these and other groups that often don't interact well with one another. And we were increasingly able to build trust and transcend the culture wars to find common ground for the common good. While we lost the election in this case, there's no reason that a faithful candidate, running at the right time and in the right district, couldn't also end up winning. Others have.

The congressional campaign was hard. But it gave me hope that things don't have to be this broken, that alternatives are not only necessary but also possible, that we can move beyond the culture wars to renew a role for faith in politics that more faithfully advances justice and healing in a broken world.

Renewing the Role of Faith in Politics

As Mahatma Gandhi wrote in his autobiography, "Those who say religion has nothing to do with politics do not know what religion means."[4] The gospel is good news for all of society, and the kingdom of God, through the lordship of Jesus Christ, does not shy away from directly engaging the powers and principalities of this world. As his followers and representatives, neither should we.

The model Jesus lived out in the Gospels, while highly instructive, is also set in a very different context than ours today, when a foreign empire was occupying biblical Israel. Political engagement takes on a new set of possibilities—and responsibilities—in a representative democracy such as the United States, where the government is constitutionally of, by, and for the people.

Each of us is empowered to be direct participants in our political system by virtue of being citizens. And so we also have a responsibility to steward our voices and votes for the common good. As the evangelical leader and political conservative Michael Gerson puts it, "In the last few decades, Christians have often done politics poorly. So do most other groups in our democracy. The answer is to do politics better. Political engagement is not a luxury."[5]

What does it look like to do politics better as followers of Christ? Here are eight aspects of our sociopolitical engagement that we need to address as part of renewing our witness and combating the growing polarization.

Stop trying to reclaim the United States as a Christian nation. Gerson describes it this way: "America was not founded as a Christian nation. . . . America was designed to be a nation where all faiths are welcomed, not one where one faith is favored."[6] This is a good thing. I don't want the church to be held responsible for all that the United States stands for and does. I also wish we would guard better against civil religion, both in how we blend patriotism into our churches and worship services—particularly around the Fourth of July—as well as in how Christianity is used in national events and political ceremonies. Similarly, we would do well to distinguish between standards that we hold to within the church and standards that we advocate for in a pluralistic society. The Constitution, not the Bible, is our social contract as a nation and the basis upon which we govern society. If we believe it's wrong for countries—even officially Islamic ones—to impose Sharia law on non-Muslims, then how can we justify imposing distinctly Christian standards on non-Christians in the United States?

Have realistic expectations. Some public figures will say anything to get ahead or elected. And sometimes we get snookered into believing their empty or unrealistic promises. There are limitations to what politics can achieve and how fast the system typically moves. Democracy is only as perfect as we are (i.e., not very perfect) and can be frustratingly slow and inefficient. But it sure beats the available alternatives. This doesn't mean we shouldn't push the system—and push it hard—toward improvement. And sometimes dramatic changes do happen in short order. But it does mean that having realistic expectations can go a long way in heading off disillusionment and cynicism.

Avoid being co-opted by a particular political party or ideology. For various reasons over the last few decades, the conservative evangelicalism I grew up in became known as a core constituency within the Republican base. This has caused tremendous damage to our public witness and has chased away many who don't identify as Republican. I pray that people of all political persuasions are welcomed into the body of Christ and that we evaluate our positions on key issues first and foremost by what the Bible teaches. Too often, however, it seems that our political ideology shapes our faith more than the other way around. For instance, many Christians have become suspicious of efforts to care for the environment because it's currently viewed as a liberal issue. This should not be the case. We should care about issues that are biblical regardless of how and where they fit with any particular party or ideology.

Overcome our fears to be motivated by love. The most frequently repeated commandment in the Bible is "do not fear." As I expressed earlier, much of our politics today is driven by fear: fear of terrorists, fear of Muslims, fear of immigrants, fear of the poor, fear of homosexuals, fear of socialism. And the list goes on. As Christians, we follow a God who is love (see 1 John 4:8) and who calls his people to be known for their love (John 13:35). And there is no fear in love (see 1 John 4:18). Much of what goes on in the public square is about building walls that weed out people who don't share the same views or identities. Being motivated by love empowers us to build bridges instead of walls and to work toward healing and reconciliation in the polarized and divisive political arena.

Rigorously seek out truth and reject misinformation. It's hard to know who to trust in politics and the media anymore. Many public figures have become experts at spinning the facts to appear in their own favor. Our numerous divisions are only further aggravated by irresponsible and inaccurate talking heads, on talk radio and cable news in particular. And then there are the dastardly forwarded emails that somehow keep making the rounds and contain all manner of vitriol, racism, and conspiracy theories. There's a fine line between effective messaging and manipulation or deception. Jesus teaches us to let our yes be yes and our no be no (see Matt. 5:37) and to be as shrewd as snakes but as innocent as doves (see Matt. 10:16). Christians should be known as people who are trustworthy and committed to very high standards of the truth.

Accept complexity as well as uncertainty. Not everything is simple or black and white. Gray areas abound. Politics thrives on sound bites and talking points, but the reality is almost always more complicated than the headlines. We are constantly faced with imperfect options operating within imperfect systems. It's a balancing act to remain principled and yet pragmatic. What would it look like to hold to our principles while accepting all the gray areas and still finding common ground on which to work together for the common good?

Respond graciously to opposition and hostility. Opposition is guaranteed in politics. How we respond, however, is up to us. Too often Christians have responded to anger with anger and to hate with hate. In the wise words of Dr. Martin Luther King Jr., however, "Darkness cannot drive out darkness; only light can do that. Hate cannot drive out hate; only love can do that."[7] We have an opportunity to set a countercultural example here by being gracious and loving toward those with whom we disagree, or who disagree with us, even if they treat us as enemies. Jesus was quite clear about what he expects of his followers: "Love your enemies, do good to those who hate you, bless those who curse you, pray for those who mistreat you. If someone slaps you on one cheek, turn to them the other side also. If someone takes your coat, do not withhold your shirt from them. . . . Then your reward will be great, and you will be children of the Most High, because he is kind to the ungrateful and wicked" (Luke 6:27–29 and 35b).

Define success by faithfulness, not effectiveness. How to define success is one of the most important questions to ask in politics. The world typically defines success by winning votes or elections. In other words, success is defined by effectiveness, which is precisely the kind of thinking that leads to believing that the ends somehow justify the means. God, however, doesn't need more effective people in this way. Rather, he's looking for faithful people. The Bible consistently calls for obedience, and out of obedience comes fruitfulness, which is true success, even if we don't always understand or recognize it at the time. We may be successful in the eyes of the world, but God measures by different standards and looks beyond the outward appearances to the heart (see 1 Sam. 16:7). Are we Christians being faithful witnesses to God by how we conduct ourselves in the public square? Is our engagement pointing people to Christ and his kingdom, both in what we advocate for and how we advocate for it?

Moving Forward

I hope the above discussion helps flesh out a new way forward for Christians in politics; one that will resonate with my generation by learning from our past and becoming more Christlike in both our ends and our means. More than additional theory, however, what we really need are new models and examples of what this looks like when lived out in the real world. How can we avoid being just another generation of angry and opinionated Christians who like to argue with and attack others in public? How can we lift up new voices that stand for an authentically independent politics and offer a compelling vision forward driven by faithfulness to God and love for our neighbors?

To that end, I'm encouraged to see newer leaders of institutions traditionally identified with the religious right, such as

Jim Daly at Focus on the Family and Russell Moore with the Southern Baptists, who are setting a more charitable and humble tone when it comes to our Christian engagement in the public square. One doesn't have to agree with them on everything in order to deeply appreciate their generally far more gracious and nuanced approach.

While new leaders like these are encouraging, we also need space for even younger generations—like us millennials—to step up and contribute in meaningful and transformational ways. Sure, we might at times be inexperienced or naïve or cynical. But that's why intergenerational collaboration and mentoring are so important. There is great potential for service and witness here if the old and young are willing to listen to each other across generational divides and create the space to grow and lead alongside one another.

Many of us long to see public service remain a worthy vocation for Christians as part of being God's people in God's world. What will it take for us to break out of the current political stereotypes and dichotomies and renew our engagement in ways that strengthen rather than compromise our faith and in ways that build rather than degrade our communities?

❯ Response by Ron Sider

Again, Ben, I agree with so much of what you say. Gridlock, cynicism about government's ability to do anything right, an unbiblically one-sided religious right—all these and more are enormously serious problems.

The political gridlock in Washington that prevents our nation from dealing effectively with a long list of serious problems is unconscionable. Republicans are right that we cannot continue indefinitely adding hundreds of billions of dollars to the national debt each year, but the Democrats rightly reject proposals to balance the budget on the backs of the poor. But instead of reasonable compromises that would both cut ineffective programs and raise additional federal revenue, Washington does nothing. You rightly lament the same problem on immigration reform. The same is true with the urgent need to invest major money in renewing the nation's infrastructure (roads, bridges, etc.). And action to avoid the devastating effects of climate change; and action to make Social Security and Medicare sustainable. And the list goes on.

You also rightly lament the narrow agenda of the religious right. I have argued for decades that if one wants to be Christian in one's politics, then one must ask: "What does the Bible say God cares about?" And the answer is quite clear. God cares about the sanctity of human life *and* economic justice for all, especially the poor. God cares about sexual integrity *and* racial justice. God cares about marriage and the family *and* peacemaking *and* creation care. I believe that the way the religious right focused narrowly on abortion, marriage, and religious freedom was finally unbiblical—even though I substantially agreed with them on those issues.

But to abandon politics in despair and cynicism would be wrong for two reasons, one theological and one pragmatic.

The theological reason is that the central Christian confession is that Jesus is Lord—Lord of every area of life. And that includes economics and politics. The New Testament dares to teach that the Risen Lord is now "the ruler of the kings of the earth" (Rev. 1:5). After the resurrection, Jesus told his disciples that all authority in heaven and earth had been given to him (Matt. 28:18). That surely includes politics! Biblical Christians who know this must live out that truth by seeking to shape politics in a way that is consistent with that confession.

The pragmatic reason against abandoning politics is a persuasive one: politics is simply too important to ignore. Political decisions shape the lives of billions of people. Think of the contribution to the well-being of the world if German Christians had not voted Hitler into office. It was politics that enabled country after country to embrace religious freedom for all its citizens. It was politics that won the vote for African Americans and women. It was politics that established and later ended apartheid in South Africa. It was politics that in the past five decades vastly expanded the number of nations that have working democracies. Just as it has in the past, politics will continue to either harm or improve the lives of billions of people around the world. One way we truly love our neighbors is through promoting the concrete political programs that improve their lives.

It is not good enough to decide that we will devote all our efforts to help our hurting neighbors with a strategy of "charitable and community service." We certainly can and should do a lot to overcome poverty and resist oppression (e.g., sexual trafficking) through voluntary faith-based organizations. I strongly endorsed the affirmation and support of faith-based organizations by presidents George W. Bush and Barack Obama. We should have more, not fewer, faith-based organizations working on all kinds of social problems.

But by themselves, private charitable approaches are simply inadequate. Vast numbers of Americans need food assistance every month to feed their families. And millions of Christians work in private (often church-related) food pantries to help meet this need. But of all the food assistance that needy Americans receive each month, only 6 percent comes from these tens of thousands of private programs. Ninety-four percent of all food aid each month comes from the government.

Or take another area. If the approximately 325,000 religious congregations in the United States decided to take over the five basic federal antipoverty programs, each congregation would need to add about $1.5 million to its annual budget.[8] Perhaps your congregation could do that. But the majority of American congregations have an annual budget of less than $100,000.

The call to place all the emphasis on voluntary, private approaches to social problems is not only impractical, it is also grounded in bad sociology and bad theology. Sociologists demonstrate clearly how persons are profoundly shaped by the socioeconomic structures in which they live. But that is not to embrace thoroughgoing sociological determinism; we do possess genuine freedom. But sociological study clearly proves that societal structures greatly shape us. And the biblical teaching on social sin (or structural injustice) helps explain how this happens.

Unfortunately, evangelicals have a highly individualistic understanding of what causes and corrects social problems. Most evangelicals are strongly inclined to think that bad personal choices cause most or all social problems. And they also believe that the solution is personal conversion and helping one person at a time.[9] It is in fact true that bad personal choices are *one* significant cause of social problems and that personal faith in Christ transforms broken persons who then begin to make better choices. But it is also true that many social problems have resulted in the past and still do result from unfair structures: legal slavery, grossly unequal educational institutions, racist laws and institutions in the United States before the civil rights movement, and apartheid institutions in South Africa, economic structures that result in people working full-time in the United States and not even earning enough to escape poverty. Evangelical failure to understand the *structural* causes of social problems is one reason why so many evangelicals wrongly imagine that "charity and community service" can solve all our social problems.[10]

Part of the problem is theological. Many evangelicals have ignored what the Bible teaches about social sin. The prophets vigorously condemned legal and economic structures that were unfair.[11] The psalmist condemned wicked rulers who "frame injustice by statute" (Ps. 94:20 ESV). And Isaiah announced God's woe on "those who decree iniquitous decrees, and the writers who keep writing oppression, to turn aside the needy from justice and to rob the poor of my people of their right" (Isa. 10:1–2 ESV). Isaiah is condemning people who write unjust laws and "bureaucrats" who implement them.

When one understands what both sociology and the Bible tell us about unfair structures that twist and distort people's lives, then one realizes that political engagement is essential. Politics is necessary to effect structural change. It took the Voting Rights Act of 1965 to abolish racist structures that prevented millions of African Americans from voting. A variety of legislative changes (i.e., some mix of raising the minimum wage, increasing the Earned Income Tax Credit, and expanding refundable child and child-care tax credits) could largely end the scandal where millions of people in the richest nation in history work full-time responsibly and cannot escape poverty. But that requires politics.

We must keep the right balance between helping one person at a time and changing structures that affect everyone. The official public policy document of the National Association of Evangelicals (NAE) (the largest evangelical network in the United States, representing about 30 million evangelicals) titled "For the Health of the Nation" gets the balance right:

> From the Bible, experience, and social analysis, we learn that social problems arise and can be substantially corrected by both personal decisions and structural changes. On the one hand, personal sinful choices contribute significantly to destructive social problems (Prov. 6:9–11), and personal conversion through faith in

Christ can transform broken persons into wholesome, productive citizens. On the other hand, unjust systems also help create social problems (Amos 5:10–15; Isa. 10:1–2) and wise structural change (for example legislation to strengthen marriage or increase economic opportunity for all) can improve society. Thus Christian civic engagement must seek to transform both individuals and institutions. While individuals transformed by the gospel change surrounding society, social institutions also shape individuals. While good laws encourage good behavior, bad laws and systems foster destructive action. Lasting social change requires both personal conversion and institutional renewal and reform.[12]

Sometimes gridlock and failure tempt us to conclude that politics is "beyond redemption." But that ignores the fact that when one takes a longer view, one can see that amazing change has happened through politics over the last fifty years. It took decades, but political engagement ended the evil of apartheid. Political activity led to the collapse of communist dictatorships across Eastern Europe—without violence! There are vastly more democratic governments in the world today than fifty years ago. Fifty years ago, authoritarian, dictatorial regimes ruled in places like South Korea, Indonesia, Brazil, and Eastern Europe. Today, democratically elected governments exist in those places. President George W. Bush's political efforts greatly expanded American economic aid to fight AIDS and malaria around the world and saved the lives of millions.

Political change takes time. Patience is essential. Simply because very good work failed to produce immigration reform after several years of sustained effort does not mean it will not eventually happen. It took William Wilberforce decades to persuade the British parliament to abolish the slave trade and decades more to end slavery itself in the British Empire. But he persisted and won. Many Americans pushed hard, without success, for more than fifty years to achieve universal health insurance for all Americans. Finally, in 2010 the (obviously less than perfect!) Affordable Care Act passed, offering the promise of health insurance to as many as 30 million more people. Politics is a slow, messy process. But the historical record clearly demonstrates that politics can achieve legislation that improves the lives of hundreds of millions of people.

One can also find encouragement in another area of significant change. Ben and I both lament the fact that for much of the last three decades, the narrow agenda of the religious right tended to dominate evangelical political thinking and action. But all through that period, there were other evangelicals promoting a broader agenda.[13] Evangelicals for Social Action (ESA), which I led, promoted a "completely pro-life" agenda. We argued that biblical Christians ought to embrace a political agenda that promoted all the things the Bible says God cares about, not just a select few. Consequently, ESA opposed abortion and economic injustice. ESA supported marriage and two-parent families as well as peacemaking, racial justice, and creation care.[14] Often we felt rather alone because that whole agenda offended people on the right *and* the left. But we persisted. And about fifteen years ago, things began to change.

From 2002 to 2004, Diane Knippers (president of the politically conservative Institute on Religion and Democracy) and I cochaired a process for the NAE. Our task was to produce a document that would outline the political platform and broad agenda of the organization. We frequently disagreed, engaged in vigorous debate, and eventually found much more common ground than we expected. The document we prepared, "For the Health of the Nation" (mentioned above), was unanimously approved in 2004 by the full board of the NAE as its official framework for its ongoing political engagement.

This document clearly rejects a narrow preoccupation with just a few issues. It explicitly declares that "the Bible makes clear that God cares a great deal about the well-being of marriage, the family, the sanctity of human life, justice for the poor, care for creation, peace, freedom, and racial justice." And the very next sentence pointedly says: "While individual persons and organizations are at times called by God to concentrate on one or two issues, *faithful evangelical civic engagement must champion a biblically balanced agenda*."[15] The document has sections on the "Sanctity of Human Life" and "The Family" but also major sections on "Justice and Compassion for the Poor," "Human Rights," "Peace," and "Protecting God's Creation."

In the decade since its approval, the NAE has provided vigorous leadership opposing cuts to government programs that empower poor people and promoting creation care and comprehensive immigration reform. In an important book, evangelical ethicist David Gushee has argued that a new "evangelical center" has emerged that now embraces this broader "biblically balanced" agenda. The NAE, *Christianity Today*, InterVarsity Press, Baker Publishing Group, ESA, the Council for Christian Colleges and Universities, evangelical development agencies, the Christian Community Development Association, the Center for Public Justice, and individuals like John Perkins, Rick Warren, and Joel Hunter are all part of this emerging evangelical center.[16] There is a new evangelical center that promotes a political agenda much broader than that of the religious right. That is surely a sign of hope—and also evidence that patience and persistence can be effective.

So what do we need going forward? Ben's eight guidelines are all excellent. We certainly need less shrill rhetoric, an end to dishonest charges and name-calling, and a new willingness to listen to each other and see the strengths in the other's position.

In the short run I do not have much hope that national politicians will start listening respectfully to opponents and overcome gridlock through sensible compromise. But Christians ought to be able to model that. Mark Rodgers (former chief of staff to Republican senator Rick Santorum) leads an off-the-record annual event that models that kind of listening among evangelicals who represent very different political views. Jim Wallis and Michael Gerson (President George W. Bush's brilliant speech writer) led a quite fruitful process that brought together "liberal" and "conservative" evangelicals to search for common ground on specific current political issues.

Evangelical congregations ought to be a place where honest, vigorous, respectful dialogue can take place among Christians who vote differently. Every congregation ought to have a study and discussion group that meets regularly to discuss current political topics. Together, Republicans, Democrats, and independents should seek to sort out biblical principles and factual data relevant to a host of specific, hotly debated, current political topics. Trying to find the strong points of those one disagrees with ought to be a rule for the dialogue. Perhaps if we had enough congregational groups of that sort, their model of civil debate might slowly even affect the public discussion.

I also think we need some new context for intergenerational dialogue over a whole host of issues. Let me illustrate with the topic of the budget deficit and the national debt. We currently spend four dollars on seniors for every one dollar we spend on children ages zero to eighteen. We run up ongoing, growing national debt to pay for things we want now but are not willing to tax ourselves to pay for.[17] As a senior, I call that intergenerational injustice—using your grandchildren's credit cards. Our children and grandchildren will have to repay the debt.

I published an article in the *Huffington Post* in February 2013 announcing that I was resigning from the American Association of Retired People (AARP) because the organization was opposing even modest increases in payments by seniors with quite large incomes. The AARP even opposed a slight increase in

Medicare payments for seniors with annual incomes of $85,000 or more. Better off seniors, I argued, ought to contribute a little more in fees and taxes so the federal government could reduce the budget deficit and spend more on children and youth.[18]

We ought to find ways for seniors like myself and millennials like Ben to engage in serious, sustained dialogue about how government expenditures should be reallocated in order to be fair to everyone. I do not know how precisely to make that happen. Perhaps some group will hear a call to organize chapters in local congregations and colleges and universities where such intergenerational dialogue could occur. Perhaps Ben and his generation will figure out a way (not on Twitter, Ben) to make it happen. I hope so.

I hope and pray that this generation of Christian youth will embrace political engagement as one important part of faithful discipleship. I hope you will embrace a biblically balanced agenda. And I trust that you will have the patience to stay the course knowing that significant political change takes years, even decades, not months or just a few years.

DISCUSSION QUESTIONS

1. Do you have any hesitancies about political involvement? If yes, what are they? If no and you are not currently involved in politics, why not?

2. Read Isaiah 58:6–12. Notice that God calls his people to deal with misery in two very different ways. Which verses talk about helping people to stick it out through their

day-to-day misery? Which verses call for eliminating the root causes of that misery? What application can you draw from this?

3. When all of society's structures benefit us, it's almost impossible to imagine them as being evil. How does Isaiah 10:1–4 give us a more objective perspective on societal structures?

4. Do you have some personal experience with social injustice or have the systems you've navigated in your life served you well? Can you give an example?

5. How would you go about helping your church start a "study and discussion group that meets regularly to discuss current political topics"? What objections do you think you'd have to overcome? What good do you think might come out of it?

8

Will We Reconcile Our Divisions Better?

BEN LOWE

Christians have become known, not for our unity, but for our divisions.

Perhaps one of the clearest ways this manifests itself is on social media. Some of the most antagonistic posts I see on Facebook and Twitter involve Christians attacking one another on any number of trending topics. Whatever the hot-button issue, we've generated quite the reputation for being disagreeable.

Disagreements, accountability, and criticism all have their place when pursued in love and humility, first in private but eventually in appropriate public forums when necessary. But a lot of what happens today is neither necessary nor loving. Instead, it often appears mean-spirited, self-righteous, and at times even gleefully divisive, focused more on tearing one another down than on building up the body of Christ. And this troubling trend extends well beyond social media to other areas of church and community life.

An Insider Perspective

Coming from a ministry family, I've experienced tremendous good and beauty in the church. We expect this from what is, after all, the visible representation of Christ in the world today. But there's also a lot of bad and ugliness too, and this can be very hurtful and disillusioning.

I've seen church members threaten to hit each other during heated congregational meetings. I've witnessed egotistical leaders misappropriate church funds for personal agendas and maneuver to take over governing boards, punishing those who stand in their way. I've listened to some of the most divisive people call passionately for unity, only to wield it as a blunt tool for coercing others to fall in line with their own agendas.

Time and again, I've watched helplessly as my father has come home beaten down after meeting with particularly hostile and manipulative elders. Then at church on Sunday I'm expected to force a smile and shake the hands of these leaders as if nothing is wrong. If I were to act out, as many of us PKs (pastor's kids) end up doing at some point, it would just get my parents into more trouble.

Don't get me wrong, I know my parents aren't perfect. And many of the people in the churches they've served are sincere and loving followers of Christ who have greatly blessed my family. Nonetheless, there are others who have attended church for many years but whose lives consistently don't show much growth or fruit. And sadly, these people sometimes successfully maneuver their way into leadership roles, which is the last place they belong.

With all the drama and vitriol, is it any surprise that many in my generation seem to be reacting against and drifting away from organized religion? Sure, there are lots of other reasons for this phenomenon. Some of it is plain laziness or a lack of discipline. And some of it is the influence of our hyperindividualistic culture that prizes independence and is typically suspicious of institutions and collective endeavors. But a big part of it also has to do with being put off by what appears to be an increasingly fragmented and dysfunctional church.

It's not hard to tell that I've been burned here. And I'm not alone. Forgiving fellow Christians and healing from the hurts that have come from within our communities is a hard but absolutely essential struggle for many of us.

What keeps me going is the sobering realization of just how much forgiveness I myself need from God and others. It's the unavoidable reality that to belong to Christ means belonging to his bride. It's the humbling recognition of what God continues to do in and through the church, in spite of our failings. It's the grateful acknowledgment that for all the hurt I've experienced, the church has also been a tremendous source of grace and healing. And it's the inspiring witness of countless brothers and sisters who quietly but steadily set an example of what it can look like to live and serve faithfully and in harmony with one another.

God's Call to Unity

The opportunity for and importance of unity among God's people is a theme that runs through the Scriptures and is emphasized in the story of Israel—which itself ended up splitting into two kingdoms—and in the life of the early church.

The apostle Paul's writings in particular are filled with admonishments for unity among the various communities of believers:

- "If it is possible, as far as it depends on you, live at peace with everyone" (Rom. 12:18).
- "For he [Christ] himself is our peace, who has made the two groups [Jews and gentiles] one and has destroyed the barrier, the dividing wall of hostility, by setting aside in his flesh the law with its commands and regulations" (Eph. 2:14–15a).
- "Make every effort to keep the unity of the Spirit through the bond of peace" (Eph. 4:3).
- "I appeal to you, brothers and sisters, in the name of our Lord Jesus Christ, that all of you agree with one another in what you say and that there be no divisions among you, but that you be perfectly united in mind and thought" (1 Cor. 1:10).
- "Don't you know that you yourselves are God's temple and that God's Spirit dwells in your midst? If anyone destroys God's temple, God will destroy that person; for God's temple is sacred, and you together are that temple" (1 Cor. 3:16–17).
- "Strive for full restoration, encourage one another, be of one mind, live in peace. And the God of love and peace will be with you" (2 Cor. 13:11).

One of Jesus's most famous prayers was for his followers to be united:

I pray also for those who will believe in me through their message, that all of them may be one, Father, just as you are in me and I am in you. . . . I have given them the glory that you gave

me, that they may be one as we are one—I in them and you in
me—so that they may be brought to complete unity. Then the
world will know that you sent me and have loved them even as
you have loved me. (John 17:20b–23)

According to Jesus, our radical unity is one of the ways that a
division-ridden and conflict-torn world would recognize that
Jesus is Lord and that we are his people.

At the same time, not all unity is created equal. The Nazis
were remarkably united in World War II, for instance, but their
unity resulted not in harmony and blessing but in great oppression and destruction. Similarly, the biblical account of the
Tower of Babel in Genesis 11 is a cautionary tale that we can
just as easily be united together for bad purposes as for good.[1]
We are called to unity that is centered on God, not on ourselves.

Where is this God-centered unity that Jesus prayed we would
share, and that in our good moments we long for? Why do we
have so much trouble building unity, and why is the body of
Christ so much more defined by our perceived differences than
our shared devotion to God?

The Church in Pieces

Not only is the church divided into different major traditions
or sects—Catholic, Protestant, Orthodox, and others—but
Protestants ourselves have taken divisions to a whole new level
by splitting into literally thousands of different denominations.

In the United States alone there are more than two hundred
Protestant and evangelical denominations today, though the
exact number is hard to define.[2] This doesn't include all the
nondenominational churches or independent megachurches
that function somewhat like mini-denominations by starting
satellite branches in other communities.

Beyond the denominational divisions, individual churches themselves experience conflicts and splits all the time. In many communities that have numerous church options—which is throughout much of America—people often hop from one church to another, depending on who has the most emotive worship experience or the trendiest pastor at any given time, moving on when the buzz wears off or trouble arises.

Our inability to get along and stick together greatly damages our witness, both among one another and before a seeking but skeptical world.

Things That Divide Us

Social psychologist Christena Cleveland has written a helpful book, *Disunity in Christ: Uncovering the Hidden Forces That Keep Us Apart*, analyzing in great depth the factors behind our divisions.[3] There are numerous sources of division in the church, and not all of them are necessary or legitimate.

Many divisions in the church today come down to demographics, such as language, age, ethnicity, culture, and socioeconomic status. It's practical for different language groups to gather in their own services. This way they can understand one another and participate more readily in the worship. There's also value for people within the same culture—particularly when they compose a minority in the surrounding society—to meet together to cultivate and celebrate their cultural heritage.

The challenge, however, is to avoid becoming social silos but instead remain fully engaged with and welcoming to others beyond the culture or language group. Sunday morning has often been lamented as one of the most racially and ethnically segregated times of the week. Shouldn't it be the opposite?

Thankfully, more congregations and leaders—such as Leroy Barber, Soong-Chan Rah, Brenda Salter McNeil, Eugene Cho, Lisa Sharon Harper, and others—are working hard within their churches, denominations, and ministries to change things. They're not doing this because it's in some way trendy or politically correct, but because it's right and healthy and beautiful. While we still have a long way to go, there are a growing number of compelling success stories of what it can look like to pursue the critical work of ethnic and racial reconciliation.

Christena Cleveland

Associate Professor of the Practice of Reconciliation and Director of the Center for Reconciliation, Duke Divinity School

In 2015, more than fifty years after Martin Luther King Jr. pronounced 11 a.m. on Sunday mornings the most segregated hour in America, the Christian church remains the most segregated institution in America. And it's not just about race! Research from political scientists Naomi Cahn and June Carbone suggests that churches are becoming more segregated along the lines of political leaning, class, theology, and pop culture.

We have reformed churches, hipster churches, Chinese churches, Pentecostal churches, emerging churches—but we rarely engage in meaningful interactions outside of our church groups. Instead, we tend to focus on the things that differentiate us from other groups, underestimate the richness that other groups bring to the kingdom of God, and foster negative attitudes about them.

But we can begin to change this pattern by talking about *ourselves* differently. By default, we often use the terms "us" and "them" when we think about and talk about different church groups. "Us" usually refers to our cultural group and "them" usually refers to a different cultural group. This is problematic because research shows that individuals automatically perceive anything that is related to *us/we* as pleasant, and anything that is related to *them/they* as unpleasant.

This research finding led the researchers to conclude that "simply using an ingroup designator (e.g., we) in thought or speech to refer to a person may automatically establish a positive predisposition toward that person, whereas an outgroup designator (e.g., they) may elicit a less positive or even negative predisposition."[4] Indeed, the mere use of the words "us" and "them" can powerfully affect how we think about others.

What if there were no *them* in the body of Christ? What if all were simply *we*?

Other demographic divides in the church, such as age and socioeconomic status, are challenges to overcome as well. There are too many churches contentedly filled mostly with college students *or* retirees, but not both; or mostly wealthy *or* lower income people, but not both.

Some divisions, though influenced by demographics, are also significantly about personal preference. For example: worship style, service length, service time, or congregational size carry significant weight in our self-absorbed and consumerist age where we often choose churches based on how they "meet our needs" or line up with what we're "shopping" for.

As social creatures, we naturally gravitate toward people and groups most like ourselves. This includes our political leanings; it can be particularly hard to build unity with those who hold to different political opinions or affiliations. We aim for unity through conformity instead of unity in diversity. Too often, we fear diversity instead of welcoming and cultivating it. This results in weaker, more vulnerable, and more myopic communities and churches.

It's the same with the rest of creation. For natural ecosystems to be healthy, they have to be made up of diverse plants and animals, all filling their niches and interacting with one another accordingly. As diversity is lost, and one species overruns and dominates the others—such as in monoculture (where only one crop at a time is cultivated in a field) or with invasive species such as the Asian carp in many rivers—beauty and health are also lost from the whole ecosystem. This leaves it less resilient and more susceptible to disease. This same instability and weakness also occurs in churches that are less diverse and more demographically homogeneous. We gravitate to churches filled with people like ourselves *and still* we fight and have trouble maintaining unity.

Cultivating Unity

This won't always be such a challenge. One day we will all be completely united before God in worship, as the apostle John witnessed in his vision that is the book of Revelation:

> After this I looked, and there before me was a great multitude that no one could count, from every nation, tribe, people and language, standing before the throne and before the Lamb. They were wearing white robes and were holding palm branches in their hands. And they cried out in a loud voice: "Salvation belongs to our God, who sits on the throne, and to the Lamb." (Rev. 7:9–10)

What a wonderful future hope and expectation! But why wait? The curtain has been torn. The dividing wall of hostility has been destroyed. Christ has given us new life in him that begins now, not just after we physically die. So what can it look like to cultivate unity among the church today?

This is a question we often ask at the Wheaton Chinese Alliance Church (WCAC), where I've been a member now for more than a decade. Saying that we're a Chinese church really isn't saying all that much. While the majority of our members are ethnically Chinese, we come from a variety of cultures and countries all across the world. We also have members of different and mixed ethnicities, including Hispanic, Caucasian, East African, and other Asian. Even among people from majority-Chinese countries there can be a significant gulf to overcome, such as between those from mainland China and Taiwan.

What makes WCAC even more unique is that we have three congregations (based on different languages) in one church. It's not just that we have three services, but we actually have a Cantonese, a Mandarin, and an English congregation, all with their distinct identities and pastors, all under one roof, seeking intentionally to function as one body.

It's a beautiful idea but, as with most worthwhile goals and endeavors, cultivating true and lasting unity in a context like WCAC is hard. It takes time, lots of grace, a willingness to listen, an ongoing commitment to investing in our common life together, and the resolve to concretely love one another sacrificially.

On a practical level, it looks like holding joint services throughout the year, sharing the pulpit among the pastors, praying consistently for and with one another, holding regular church-wide lunches, and more. It involves having an all-church budget, governing board, and congregational meetings. It means we invest a lot of energy talking and working on ideas to help build relationships and foster greater understanding, love, and unity. And it means we often fail and have to learn from our mistakes and find ways to move forward together.

As missionaries know only too well from working across cultures, it can take living and worshiping among one another for years before trust is slowly established and relational breakthroughs can take place. A critical part of building unity is also not just about what we agree or disagree on, but how we go about disagreeing and resolving conflicts when they arise. Which is why we've even had Sunday school classes on learning how to handle conflict and build unity. Such initiatives can go a long way in preparing communities for the inevitable issues that arise from doing life together.

What I've learned from my experience at WCAC is that a more accurate metaphor for describing the unity we seek is not a melting pot, where everything blends into one indistinguishable mass of glop, but a stew or curry where the various ingredients retain their unique and recognizable aspects while mingling together to create a rich and distinctive dish.

Beyond the local church level, the importance of cultivating unity also extends to the worldwide church. For some time now the West has been the center of Christianity. That's changing quickly as the church in other regions of the world continues to grow and take on greater leadership. How do we better collaborate with and make room for our brothers and sisters globally? And what does unity look like in a world where many Christians are suffering through great persecution while others are enjoying significant privilege?

This is why organizations such as Voice of the Martyrs, along with international networks such as the World Evangelical Alliance, and international gatherings such as the Lausanne Movement, have vital roles to play in the health of the church.

Irreconcilable Differences

All the divisions discussed up to this point (language, age, ethnicity, culture, and socioeconomic status) are things that can and should be overcome. However, when it comes to divisions that result from either *unrepentant sin* or *diverging doctrine*, it can be far less clear how to move forward. These final two categories are perhaps the most challenging.

Yes, we can repent from sin and be restored. And yes, we can often find ways to work through doctrinal differences and either agree to disagree or else reach some common ground. A good proverb to practice here is "In essentials unity; in nonessentials liberty; in all things charity."

But what happens when we come to a critical impasse and no solution is in sight? What if someone is actively divisive and refuses to change? Or what if someone is abusive—whether verbally, emotionally, physically, sexually, or spiritually—and is causing great damage to others and the church, and resists discipline? How should they be dealt with? As the apostle Paul advises Titus: "But avoid foolish controversies and genealogies and arguments and quarrels about the law, because these are unprofitable and useless. Warn a divisive person once, and then warn them a second time. After that, have nothing to do with them. You may be sure that such people are warped and sinful; they are self-condemned" (Titus 3:9–11).

And what happens on a more systemic or corporate level when deep differences in theology and doctrine arise that cut closer to the core of the community's identity? Are diverging positions on homosexuality grounds for splitting a church or denomination? What about views on divorce, or women in leadership, or the doctrines of salvation and hell?

Given the importance of unity, what is worth dividing up over and what can be accommodated? Navigating between the tension of guarding orthodoxy (however that's defined) and extending grace to those who disagree with us (whatever that looks like) is often not easy or obvious. And, if irreconcilable conflicts do lead to a lasting split, then how should a church or community go about that hard process in a way that would be most honoring to God and loving to one another?

Building Bridges

A final question on the topic of unity is on how we relate to those we are separated from. Too often we just cut each other off and go our different ways. But is that the right approach? How can we foster some level of reconciliation and collaboration even when major underlying differences remain unresolved?

This can take on many forms. For instance, Christians remain deeply divided over our positions on war and violence. Some denominations describe themselves as "peace churches" and hold to the principles of Christian pacifism, while others advocate for just war theory, and yet others refrain from taking an official position at all. In spite of deeply held moral and theological positions here, most Christians on any side would still accept those who disagree with them as also being true (if somewhat misguided) followers of Christ. So how should churches and individuals on opposing sides of such issues relate to one another?

Or, for the denominations and churches that have already split up over the role of women in leadership or human sexuality or a combination of multiple factors and disagreements, what could it look like to build bridges with one another so that some relationship and unity can be restored over time?

This question applies as well on a larger scale to the major branches of Christianity—Catholic, Protestant, and Orthodox. Some have been working hard to build bridges back between these traditions, such as John Armstrong through the ACT3 Network and Unity Factor Forums (www.act3network.com), and Wes Granberg-Michaelson, who formerly served as general

secretary for the Reformed Church in America and wrote *Unexpected Destinations: An Evangelical Pilgrimage to World
Christianity.*[5]

What's the role and value of ecumenicalism in such cases,
and how far can we go in recognizing our fundamental and
powerful areas of unity without glossing over our very real
disagreements?

In all these areas, unity is a biblical priority, but conflicts
and divisions are an ongoing reality. On one hand we want to
defend what we believe to be true about God, life, and eternity.
On the other hand, however, we want to love one another well
and be the bride that Christ will be returning for any day. We've
often walked this challenging tension very poorly; how can we
do this better moving forward?

Response by Ron Sider

I hope I do not begin to sound like a broken record. But again
in this chapter, I agree overwhelmingly with what Ben says. He
vividly and powerfully describes a huge problem. And he cites
the many strong New Testament texts that summon Christians
to unity. Finally, at the end of the chapter, he pointedly raises
two of the toughest questions.

Nothing more powerfully summons us to struggle against
division in the church than our Lord's final prayer that his followers "may be brought to complete unity. Then the world will
know that you sent me" (John 17:23). If the love and unity in the
church is going to convince the world that Jesus came from the

Father, our unity cannot be some invisible, "spiritual" unity. It must be visible if the world is to see it. When we compare Christ's prayer to the ghastly divisions among Christ's followers, one can only weep.

Pondering that call today prompts me to reflect on my seventy-six years of life in local congregations and, as I grew older, in interdenominational, ecumenical activities. I grew up in a congregation in the Brethren in Christ Church—a tiny denomination with Anabaptist, Pietist, and Wesleyan roots. Our understanding of who was included in the circle of faithful Christians certainly did not include Catholics, Orthodox Christians, and theologically liberal Protestants. But my small denomination did participate in larger interdenominational structures in the Mennonite, Wesleyan Holiness, and evangelical traditions.

Any experience of racial diversity in the church would have to wait. My rural farm community and church in southern Ontario (Canada) was all white. But after graduate school, as I began teaching at Messiah College's inner-city campus in (overwhelmingly black) North Philadelphia, my wife and I attended an almost entirely black Presbyterian church for seven years in order to learn and even make a tiny statement about the widespread racial segregation of the church. Then from 1975 to 1980, we were part of a house church (Jubilee Fellowship) of young, white evangelical radicals vigorously committed to racial justice. But in spite of the fact that the neighborhood where we lived was more than 50 percent African American, our circle of young, white radicals championing racial and economic justice, simple lifestyles, and communal sharing did not seem to be attractive to our black neighbors!

When Jubilee Fellowship began to dissolve in 1980, our family joined an exciting interracial Mennonite congregation located in an all-black section of North Philadelphia. For several years, the congregation brought together significant numbers of black and white Christians, and the interracial congregation seemed to work. But then racial tension and conflict flared up, and after several painful years, denominational leaders suggested that the white members should leave. That experience was a very painful one, but it taught me how very hard it is to develop a truly integrated congregation where African American and European American Christians can work together as equals who deeply respect, trust, and cooperate with each other.

Not until the year 2000 did my wife, Arbutus, and I enjoy a congregation that began to look significantly like the church that Revelation 7:9–10 depicts gathered in heaven. Oxford Circle Mennonite Church (located in a lower-income, extremely ethnically diverse section of Philadelphia) is truly interracial. Perhaps 50 percent of the congregation is white, 25 percent African American, 20 percent Hispanic, and the rest a mix of Asians, Palestinians, and others! There must be at least a dozen interracial couples. The senior pastor is an African American man married to a Latina, and the other pastor is a white woman. African Americans, Hispanics, and European Americans are involved in every level of the congregation's life and leadership.

And it is working! I have lived too long and know too much about the depth of white-black distrust grounded in our terribly painful, racist history to expect a racially diverse congregation to work well. But it does. In our fourteen years there, we have not had any substantial racial conflict. I have never in my whole life been so happy about my local congregation. Of course the local congregation is far from perfect. But it is part of a small but growing number of local congregations that demonstrate that the racial segregation that Ben rightly laments is slowly being overcome.

I have also had the joy of experiencing growing interdenominational dialogue and understanding in my lifetime. In 1973, I coordinated the meeting of evangelical leaders that issued the

Chicago Declaration of Evangelical Social Concern. Almost immediately, ecumenical leaders contacted us to express their delight with finding evangelicals who cared about peace and justice. Several two-day ecumenical dialogues soon followed, and I was invited to the Nairobi Assembly of the World Council of Churches in 1975. In the 1980s and beyond, I frequently found that it was Catholics who most closely embraced the "completely pro-life" political agenda of my organization, Evangelicals for Social Action.

In early September 2001, I attended the first meeting of what eventually became Christian Churches Together in the USA (CCT). Up to that point, mainline Protestants, Orthodox Christians, and Christians from African American denominations participated in the National Council of Churches, but Catholics and evangelicals/Pentecostals did not. In that September 2001 meeting, we asked whether the time was ripe for a new ecumenical table that could bring us all together. Over the course of several annual meetings, we decided the answer was yes. I worked hard to help encourage evangelicals/Pentecostals to participate. And for the first time in American history, all five families—historic Protestants, Orthodox Christians, African Americans, Roman Catholics, and evangelicals/Pentecostals—came together at the same ecumenical table. I felt privileged to participate in what I believed was a tiny but significant step toward obeying our Lord's prayer in John 17.

Over the years, I have more and more wanted to emphasize the things that unite rather than the things that divide various parts of the Christian family. There continue to be major theological disagreements among Catholics, Orthodox Christians, and Protestants that no one knows how to resolve. But I prefer to stress what all Christians have in common. Catholics, Orthodox Christians, and Protestants (at least those who still believe their official creeds) all affirm:

- God is Father, Son, and Holy Spirit, three persons in one God.
- Jesus is true God and true man.
- Jesus's life, death on the cross, and resurrection provide the only way to salvation for all people.
- Jesus rose bodily from the dead on the third day.
- The Bible is God's unique, authoritative special revelation.

Anyone who truly affirms those things is my beloved sister or brother in Christ even though we continue to have significant theological disagreements.

But that still leaves unanswered Ben's question about how much theological disagreement is acceptable within a congregation, denomination, or ecumenical body. Catholics and evangelicals have major disagreements about issues like the Eucharist, Mary, and the role of the pope (to name a few!). Evangelical Christians disagree among themselves—for example, about predestination versus free will and just war versus pacifism. Many historic Protestant leaders doubt that Jesus is the only way to salvation. Some even no longer affirm the deity of Christ or Jesus's bodily resurrection. So what should we do?

I believe that our ongoing theological disagreements result from our sin and finitude. If all Christians were fully open to what the Bible and the Holy Spirit want to teach us, we would be able to resolve these theological differences. We would all attain that "unity in the faith" that Paul wants (Eph. 4:13). That means that the continuing existence of different theological denominations flows from our sin and displeases our Lord. We must continue to repent of our sinful disobedience and persist in vigorous efforts to reach theological agreement and visible unity.

But what do we do until we are able to reach that agreement and unity? There has been progress on some significant areas of historic disagreement between Catholics and Protestants.[6] Today we seldom say the awful things about each other that were still common when I was young. Widespread evangelical admiration for Pope Francis is just one illustration of the fact that many on both sides recognize and embrace each other as committed Christians.

But major theological disagreements persist. And I do not see much likelihood (short of sweeping, miraculous divine intervention!) that we will be able to resolve these differences in the next few decades.

I believe this means we must reluctantly accept the need for different denominations even as we confess that their ongoing existence results from our sinful inability to listen fully to the Word and Spirit. Christians have been trying to understand the relationship of divine activity and the freedom of the will for millennia. The difference between Calvinists who affirm double predestination and Arminians who believe that the free response of persons rather than God's eternal decree shapes our eternal destiny is a major disagreement. So is the dispute between pacifists who say Jesus taught his followers never to kill and just war Christians who insist that sometimes, reluctantly, Christians must kill to promote peace and justice. And major disagreements between Protestants and Catholics are at least as substantial.

I believe that for the foreseeable future, we should confess that different denominations are necessary, even though they result from our sinfulness. We sadly need denominations (and of course their many congregations) that embrace double predestination and reject an Arminian affirmation of free will—and other denominations that believe the reverse. The same is true for big issues like just war versus pacifism, the bodily presence of Christ in the Eucharist versus his spiritual presence, and many others.

The inclination of many people today is just to ignore these differences and abandon any attempt to base church membership or leadership on acceptance of one view or the other on these historic disagreements. I think that is a fundamental mistake. Mennonites (unless they change their minds on what they believe Jesus taught about killing) should continue to live out the belief that members in good standing should not accept belief in just war. And congregations and denominations in the just war tradition should do the same.

But the fact that we have Calvinist and Arminian, pacifist and "just war" denominations need not—dare not!—result in harsh attack or denial that the other denomination is Christian. To help with that, we need, in addition to denominations, larger ecumenical tables that bring together broader groups of Christians from different denominations.

The World Evangelical Alliance (WEA), which represents about 600 million evangelicals and Pentecostals in national evangelical fellowships around the world, is one such group. Member denominations differ over infant versus adult baptism, predestination versus free will, pacifism versus just war, and more. But they all believe in the Trinity, the deity and humanity of Jesus, Jesus as the only way to salvation, Jesus's bodily resurrection, the importance of evangelism, and the Bible as God's special, fully reliable revelation as the supreme guide for faith and practice. Across the many theological divisions that continue unresolved, everyone in the WEA accepts the others as genuine Christians, brothers and sisters in Christ. And they continue to find ways to work together.

An even broader ecumenical table is present in Christian Churches Together, which brings together denominations from five families (historic Protestants, Orthodox Christians, African Americans, Catholics, and evangelicals/Pentecostals). In CCT, the theological affirmations that all accept are less extensive. Every denomination and organization joining CCT must affirm that Jesus Christ is "God and Savior according to the Scriptures" and

"worship and serve the one God, Father, Son, and Holy Spirit."
That brief theological statement does not say Jesus is the only
way to salvation or specify what CCT member denominations believe about the Bible. There would be major disagreement among
various members of CCT on these and other issues. But I believe
strongly that anyone who affirms that God is Father, Son, and
Holy Spirit, and that Jesus Christ is God is my Christian brother
or sister. I want to affirm our oneness in Christ and work together
where we can, even as we continue to debate numerous important
theological issues. Stressing where we agree more than where we
still disagree is one important way that we continue to repent of
our sinful inability to move beyond denominations that divide us.

There is no global body comparable to CCT. But we need one.
Fortunately, the Global Christian Forum represents movement
toward that goal.

This framework—both sadly acknowledging the need for different denominations and also strongly embracing broader ecumenical tables that unite the one body of Christ—still leaves us
with very hard questions. We cannot avoid continuing to discuss
what differences are significant enough to warrant different denominations. Please God, may we no longer divide denominations
over the petty things (e.g., dress, dancing, or a pretribulation vs.
a posttribulation rapture) that often provoked church splits in
the past. Sadly, however, it will not always (perhaps only infrequently) be clear what issues are basic enough to require different denominations and what disagreements are insignificant
enough to allow diversity. Today, the issue of whether Christians
should accept or reject same-sex practice poses this question very
clearly. Some Christians today believe that a gay couple (of committed Christians) in an exclusive, lifelong sexual relationship
should be fully affirmed. Others strongly disagree. Is this issue
important enough to have denominations choose one position
or the other and apply appropriate decisions about membership

and leadership? I am inclined to think this issue is that important, although I respect those Christians who disagree. But those who say separate denominations are needed on this issue must certainly accept at ecumenical tables like CCT those Christian denominations that embrace and affirm gay Christian couples.[7]

Church unity that is visible—visible to unbelievers who need to be convinced that Jesus came from the Father—is the only way to be faithful to our Lord's final prayer. Sadly, for a time, we must confess that our ongoing sin prevents us from transcending the different denominations that divide us. But we must renew and redouble our efforts and prayers to seek the visible unity Christ desires.

What about Ben's question about church discipline? That has been largely lost in the contemporary church in the West. And history shows that it has often been exercised in ways that were harsh and legalistic—and led to ghastly splits in the church. So should we quietly forget about church discipline? No, for two reasons. First because Jesus commands it and the early church practiced it. And second, church discipline has historically been an important part of most Christian traditions.

Jesus is quite clear:

> If your brother or sister sins, go and point out their fault, just between the two of you. If they listen to you, you have won them over. But if they will not listen, take one or two others along, so that "every matter may be established by the testimony of two or three witnesses." If they still refuse to listen, tell it to the church; and if they refuse to listen even to the church, treat them as you would a pagan or a tax collector. (Matt. 18:15–17)

And St. Paul certainly commanded and practiced what Matthew 18 demands. He ordered the Corinthian church to expel a man engaged in sexual immorality (1 Cor. 5:1–13).

Historically, almost all branches of the Christian church have practiced church discipline: Catholics, Orthodox, Calvinists, Methodists, Anabaptists, and more. When I, as a youth, joined my church with its strong Anabaptist and Wesleyan roots, I had to promise as part of the membership liturgy to practice Matthew 18. Church discipline was a central practice for Methodists in their first hundred years when they enjoyed explosive growth. In their weekly "class meetings," John Wesley directed that they should ask, "Where have you sinned this week?"

In 1972, at a time when historic Protestant denominations were declining and evangelicals were growing, Dean M. Kelly, a key staff person for the more liberal National Council of Churches, wrote a book called *Why Conservative Churches Are Growing*.[8] His answer was in part: because they still practice church discipline! Our primary concern, of course, is not church growth. It is biblical fidelity. And that requires that even in hyperindividualistic North America, our churches should seek to recover the practice of church discipline. I know that sounds scary. I know church discipline has often been practiced very badly in the past. I pray that we will never repeat the petty legalism and harsh (even lethal) punishment that too often was a part of earlier practice.

But there is a better, more gentle, loving way to do it. Galatians 6 specifies the proper spirit and tone: "Brothers and sisters, if someone is caught in a sin, you who live by the Spirit should restore that person gently. But watch yourselves, or you also may be tempted. Carry each others' burdens" (Gal. 6:1–2). Church discipline should not mean law courts and harsh punishment. It should mean, first, private weeping and prayer for a sister or brother who is going astray—and then the several steps that Jesus outlined. At each stage, the central message is a gentle, loving plea to turn from sin and embrace the forgiveness and transformation that the Father longs to bestow. But a faithful church will not allow contemporary individualism to stop it from taking the third step Jesus outlined. If the person refuses to repent and demonstrates the intention of continuing in sin, then the church must lovingly insist that the person cannot continue in good standing in the congregation. But even this last step is not a penalty. Rather, it is a final, desperate plea to the person to return to the open arms of our loving and holy God.[9] That, it appears, was precisely what happened in Corinth when the church followed Paul's instructions and removed a sinner from their midst. In his second letter, Paul urged the congregation to forgive and comfort the repentant person and "reaffirm your love for him" (2 Cor. 2:7–8).

I pray that the visible unity of the one body of Christ will be a much higher priority for younger Christians than for my generation (which has already seen quite substantial progress). But simply ignoring important theological differences or persistent sin is not the way to achieve it. Relativism and radical individualism are not the path to the unity our Lord desires. Rather, all parts of the Christian church must get to know one another better, study the Bible together, revisit and reassess our often disobedient history together, emphasize more the central truths that we all embrace, and plead with the Lord of the whole church to lead us into a new unity that today seems almost impossible.

DISCUSSION QUESTIONS

1. How diverse is your own church in terms of ethnicity, age, and economic status? Is the level of diversity comparable

to that of the surrounding neighborhood? Are certain kinds of people underrepresented in your church?

2. Acts 11:19–26 gives us a behind-the-scenes look at the development of the first multiethnic church. Read this passage and carefully note how it came about, how we know it was potentially explosive, how the leadership responded to this unplanned development, and how it ultimately exalted Jesus.

3. If you were to use the Antioch church (described in Acts 11) as a way to understand your own church's timeline of development, where would you place your church on that timeline? How might this understanding be helpful to you in moving forward?

4. Wisdom—being wise about what the Bible says, able to tell right from wrong—is often considered a vital prerequisite for leadership. James says that real wisdom "is characterized by getting along with others. It is gentle and reasonable, overflowing with mercy and blessings, not hot one day and cold the next, not two-faced. You can develop a healthy, robust community that lives right with God and enjoy its results *only* if you do the hard work of getting along with each other, treating each other with dignity and honor" (3:17–18 Message). How can this kind of wisdom become more prominent in your own leadership?

5. Jesus prayed that his followers would be "brought to complete unity. Then the world will know that you sent me" (John 17:23). Ron emphasizes that since this unity is going to give the world evidence to believe, it must be visible so that the world can see it. To what extent is your church's unity giving the world evidence to believe?

9

Will We Recover Our Responsibility for God's Creation?

BEN LOWE

There's a well-known saying that we don't inherit the earth from our ancestors; we borrow it from our children.[1] The earth that previous generations have borrowed from us, however, is being left in many ways worse off than ever. Why aren't we doing more to take care of creation?

Remarkable progress has been made across numerous societal fronts, including education, health care, communication, transportation, consumer choice, and more. But in each case we also find that much of this growth has been inequitable and unsustainable. Too often it has come at a steep cost to other people, creatures, and places that have been and are being adversely impacted by our production, pollution, and waste.

The status quo is working well for a number of us in the developed world—at least for now—but what we truly need is a holistic and sustainable approach that benefits all people, particularly those living on the margins, as well as the rest of creation.

Transforming the Status Quo

It's increasingly and painfully clear that business as usual is not the answer for my generation. We're groaning from a host of interconnected social and environmental problems, and nearly every environmental indicator points toward trouble for our shared future on God's good but groaning earth:

- 7 million premature deaths every year are linked to indoor and outdoor air pollution.[2]
- 2,200 children under the age of five die of diarrheal diseases daily, with lack of clean water contributing to 88 percent of all diarrheal diseases.[3]
- 805 million people in the world do not have enough to eat on any given day, and poor nutrition is responsible for the deaths of 3.1 million children under the age of five each year.[4]
- 2.6 billion people depend directly on agriculture for survival, but arable land is being lost at 30 to 35 times the historical rate, and more than half the land currently being cultivated is experiencing moderate to severe soil degradation.[5]
- More than a third of all currently assessed species are threatened with extinction, and we've lost 6 million hectares of primary forest every year since 2000 alone.[6]
- Energy-driven conflicts continue to spread, with many of our military leaders and experts warning that climate

change is fast becoming one of our greatest global security threats, as well as a major driver of forced human migration.[7]

- Diverse and far-reaching effects of climate disruption are putting additional strain on all the above areas as well as on many other natural and human systems. For instance, sea-level rise continues to render coastal communities—including many of the world's major cities—vulnerable to flooding and saltwater intrusion. And, because of all the excess carbon dioxide that the oceans have been absorbing, they've become 30 percent more acidic since the industrial revolution (which harms corals and many other commercially and ecologically important species that form calcium carbonate shells).[8]

Granted, things weren't perfect before this. And none of us sets out intending to destroy the earth. Nonetheless, with rapidly progressing technology and the struggle to better support a growing population on a finite planet, along with our corrupt human condition and broken societal structures, we're making things decisively worse.

More technology isn't quite the simple answer that some are hoping for. It may make us more powerful, but it doesn't guarantee that we'll use our greater power only for good. As history repeatedly shows, even with good intentions there's no guarantee that we'll be able to wield technology with enough skill and wisdom to avoid harmful side effects.

Consider the unintended societal and ecological damage caused by the countless dams and canals built by the US Army Corps of Engineers last century, in an ill-conceived attempt to drain wetlands, control water flow, and create new land for agriculture and development. After numerous problems and flooding disasters, we're now in the expensive and time-consuming process of trying to undo many of those projects, such as across the Everglades in South Florida.

We should still strive for and celebrate technological breakthroughs for all the good they can offer. At the same time, however, we need to remember soberly that the greater the technology, the greater the stakes for both good and bad. And the stakes are high for the billions of us sharing the earth today.

So how much worse will we let things get before we find better and more biblically faithful ways forward? How many more people will waste away from hunger and dirty water? How many more species will be lost forever due to human action? How many more wars will be fought over our apparently insatiable appetite for energy and natural resources? Inheritances are meant to be a blessing; this one is starting to seem like more of a curse. And the church too often has been found lacking here.

A Blind Spot

For many Christians today, creation care is still not an integral part of our discipleship and witness. Many of our churches still aren't teaching it, many of our families aren't modeling it, and many of us aren't practicing it in our lifestyles.

As I've mentioned in earlier chapters, I grew up in a loving evangelical home. I've worshiped in more than a hundred churches (my family traveled a lot as missionaries) and have listened to well over a thousand sermons. Yet it wasn't until I was nineteen years old that I first heard about creation care. Dr. Vince Bacote, a professor at Wheaton College, was preaching at my church as a guest and spoke about the stewardship mandate from Genesis 2:15.

That sermon was a paradigm shift for me. I grew up loving nature and seizing every opportunity I had to go hiking, fishing, and camping. My free time as a kid was spent exploring trails in local forest preserves, chasing after mudskippers on tidal flats, climbing trees, going camping with friends, and more. But until my freshman year of college I had never clearly connected my love of God's creation with my love of God the Creator. I had read the Bible from cover to cover but had developed a glaring blindspot when it came to the many passages having to do with creation and our role and relationship within it. Finally being able to integrate my passion for God's creation with my biblical faith was a life-changing step forward in my walk with Christ.

The Church's Witness

My experience of growing up in church with creation care being a blind spot is sadly all too common these days. This has not always been the case.

Throughout history, Christians often have been leaders in stewarding creation, protecting habitats, conserving resources, treating animals with compassion, and championing scientific discovery and sustainable development. After all, Pope Francis chose to be named after St. Francis of Assisi, the patron saint of ecology. William Wilberforce, an evangelical politician in eighteenth- and nineteenth-century Great Britian, is known not just for his remarkable leadership in abolishing the slave trade but also for cofounding the Royal Society for the Prevention of Cruelty to Animals (RSPCA).

Even over the last fifty years, as the church developed more of a reputation for being suspicious of environmental initiatives, groups such as the Au Sable Institute, A Rocha, and the Evangelical Environmental Network (EEN) have presented clear and compelling alternatives to this stereotype. Numerous Christians such as Dr. Simon Stuart of the International Union for

Conservation of Nature, Sir John Houghton of the Intergovernmental Panel on Climate Change, Sir Ghillean Prance of the Royal Botanical Gardens-Kew, Larry Schweiger of the National Wildlife Federation, and many others have risen to the very top of their conservation and environmental fields worldwide, demonstrating that faith in Christ should empower and not detract us from effective service and leadership in these fields.

Too often, however, such exceptions are just that—exceptions instead of the norm. In my work with EEN, I interact with numerous Christians and churches that range from being apathetic and disengaged to being downright hostile and opposed to caring for creation.

I recently met with the pastor of a large, wealthy evangelical church who told me upfront that creation care is a "distraction from the true priorities of the church." Much of the rest of our conversation was about how his congregants struggle with issues of sexual morality (such as pornography and premarital sex) and how creation care thus really didn't rank on his list of concerns. I've heard variations of this polite statement a lot through the years: "Interesting that you care about environmental issues, but that's not part of our mission/focus/priorities/concern/purpose." Then there was the woman who came up to me after I spoke at a large missions conference and publicly declared me a heretic who had been deceived by the devil into being an agent of the liberal, godless environmental movement.

The church's reputation regarding environmental issues is so widespread that many environmentalists view the church en bloc as being opposed to their efforts, and are surprised when they find Christians who do care. EEN's president, Rev. Mitch Hescox, was once invited to speak to the board of a major environmental organization and was described, because of his faith, as being the most "exotic" speaker they had ever had. How sad that a Christian who cares about creation is viewed as exotic!

We're well known for being fixated on the creation-versus-evolution debate. But, as I hear from folks outside the faith: "You Christians argue about creation versus evolution to no end, but then treat the earth as if it doesn't matter. If you really believe your God created this world, then shouldn't you treat it better?"

Yes, we should.

Our Biblical Responsibility

What should our attitude be toward the environment? What is our biblical role in creation, and why is it important for the church to be more engaged?

The Bible has much to say here—much more than can be covered in this chapter. One central principle is that we are created as part of creation but with a distinct capacity and role: to be its caretakers. Genesis 1 reveals that everything was made *in its own image*: the fish in the likeness of fish, the birds in the likeness of birds, and the livestock and wild animals in their respective likenesses. Everything was created in *its own image* except, that is, for us:

> Then God said, "Let us make mankind *in our image*, *in our likeness*, so that they may rule over the fish in the sea and the birds in the sky, over the livestock and all the wild animals, and over all the creatures that move along the ground." So God created mankind *in his own image*, *in the image of God* he created them; male and female he created them. God blessed them and said to them, "Be fruitful and increase in number; fill the earth and subdue it. Rule over the fish in the sea and the birds in the sky and over every living creature that moves on the ground." (Gen. 1:26–28, emphasis added)

Gabriel Salguero

President, National Latino Evangelical Coalition

As an evangelical, I believe that "I am my brother's and sister's keeper." This means that I have a moral responsibility to protect those closest to me, as well as my "neighbors" around the world. One of the greatest mistakes we've made is failing to show others how climate change and other environmental degradations affect people and their daily lives. While I believe we must protect all of creation, I also recognize that there is a human story here that too often goes untold.

Studies have shown that one in ten Latino children suffers from asthma (including my own son), and one in two Latinos lives in areas with unhealthy ozone levels. These conditions are worsened by power plant pollution and the higher temperatures caused by climate change from the carbon they emit.

We also know that climate change contributes to stronger storms. Based on my own experience helping with Hurricane Sandy relief in New York City, I've seen firsthand how these disasters disproportionately impact the poor. This is not isolated to the United States. Stronger storms and changing weather patterns are disrupting the lives of our brothers and sisters throughout the world, especially Latinos in Central and South America, who often lack the resources to prepare and rebuild.

Climate change has often been pushed aside because it has seemed too complicated or difficult to solve, but we have a God-given obligation to protect our neighbors and future generations. As God's people, let's take positive steps to lead on climate action in our homes, churches, and communities. Let's ensure that the costs of our inaction do not get passed down to our children and the most vulnerable. We can and must do better.

Humans are distinct within creation in that we are made not in our own image but in God's. As God's image-bearers, we're his agents and representatives. He's privileged us with the important work of reflecting *his image* to all creation and carrying out *his will* across the face of the earth. Being God's image-bearers is what most definitively distinguishes us from the birds, giraffes, other primates, and all the rest of creation. It's what gives us both the capacity and authority to order and govern the world in ways that glorify the Creator. It's what it means to be human. Three relevant implications arise from being God's image-bearers.

1. *We are created to be stewards.* We tend to talk a lot in our churches about stewardship, but mostly we're referring to stewardship of our money or time. But that's not where this discussion should end. One of the core values of the Christian and Missionary Alliance, an evangelical denomination that I'm a member of, is that everything we have belongs to God; we are his stewards. Imagine what it would look like if we lived fully into this truth throughout every area of life!

Everything we have belongs to God—including the earth and all its species, people, places, and resources—and we have been given the responsibility to exercise good stewardship for God's sake (see Gen. 1; 2:15; Ps. 8). What does this mean for how we consume energy, how we shop, how we eat, how we dispose of waste, how we protect nature, how we cultivate our yards and gardens, and so much more? How can we recover a holistic practice of biblical stewardship that empowers the church to lead in caring for our neighbors and the rest of God's creation?

2. *We are commanded to love.* God is love and to bear God's image is to be a people of love (see 1 John 4:8). When the Pharisees tested Jesus by asking him to identify the greatest commandment, he replied: "'Love the Lord your God with all your heart and with all your soul and with all your mind.' This is

the first and greatest commandment. And the second is like it: 'Love your neighbor as yourself.' All the Law and the Prophets hang on these two commandments" (Matt. 22:37–40).

How can we claim to love God if we don't treat his creation with love? I recently heard an art student describe God as a master artist who created a beautiful and intricate piece of art and gifted it to his children to enjoy and look after. If his children really love him, then they will share their father's delight in the magnificent art. They will cherish and protect it; and if it's ever damaged, then they will share in his pain and sadness.

Similarly, how can we claim to love our neighbor if we don't address the environmental problems that they're being impacted by? As one of my college professors put it: When the land isn't healthy, people aren't healthy. When the air is polluted, people develop asthma, cancer, and other respiratory diseases. When the water is contaminated, people suffer from diarrhea, parasites, and other illnesses. We are inextricably dependent on the rest of creation. A critical way to love our neighbor is by ensuring that they have access to clean air, pure water, healthy food, and a stable ecosystem in which to thrive.

3. *We are called to reconcile*.[9] Environmental problems are also moral and spiritual problems requiring moral and spiritual solutions. In his book *Jesus Brand Spirituality*, Pastor Ken Wilson shares the following quote from eminent environmentalist Dr. James "Gus" Speth:

> I used to think that if we threw enough good science at the environmental problems, we could solve them. I was wrong. The main threats to the environment are not biodiversity loss, pollution, and climate change, as I once thought. They are selfishness and greed and pride. And for that we need a spiritual and cultural transformation, something we scientists don't know much about.[10]

Dr. Speth is right. To put it precisely, the root of all these problems is sin. Therefore, what we ultimately need is a solution to sin.

The Bible speaks directly to this. In the beginning, God created the world in a state of shalom, with harmony and right relationships flourishing between all things in the Garden of Eden—within ourselves, between us and one another, between us and creation, within creation, and between creation and God. When humans rebelled, however, our relationship with God was fractured and all other relationships down the line were also broken as a result. Romans 8:19–22 described almost two thousand years ago what our science today is quantifying: that all of creation is groaning from the effects of our sin. This is the bad news.

The good news is that God has not given up on his creation. The rest of the Bible is the story of God saving the world from sin, first by working through the law and a chosen people known as the Israelites, and then ultimately by working through his only Son, Jesus Christ: "For God was pleased to have all his fullness dwell in him [Jesus], and through him to reconcile to himself all things, whether things on earth or things in heaven, by making peace through his blood, shed on the cross" (Col. 1:19–20).

Christ is not only the creator and sustainer of all things but also the reconciler of the same. By dying on the cross Jesus paid the price of our sin and thus opened the door for all things to be reconciled into a right relationship with God, and therefore also into right relationship with one another. Everything that was broken as a result of our sin is to be restored. Or, as one of my friends puts it, "the cross is for all of the fall."

Joining God in this great work of reconciliation and restoration is the mission of the church. As the Lausanne Movement—the worldwide network for evangelical leaders and churches founded by Billy Graham and John Stott—puts it in their 2010 definitive statement on contemporary Christian mission, *The Cape Town Commitment*:

> Integral mission means discerning, proclaiming, and living out the biblical truth that the gospel is God's good news, through the cross and resurrection of Jesus Christ, for individual persons, and for society, and for creation. All three are broken and suffering because of sin; all three are included in the redeeming love and mission of God; all three must be part of the comprehensive mission of God's people.[11]

We are called to be both recipients and agents of Christ's reconciliation, and that reconciliation includes both people and the rest of creation. This needs to be worked out at every level of our lives and society.

How can we reconcile the often-dueling priorities of human development and nature conservation so that we're able to both care for people and sustain the rest of creation at the same time? What does it look like to help restore right relationships in how we use water, food, energy, and otherwise live on and impact the earth? In other words, how can we as both individuals and communities have a smaller negative impact on creation and our neighbors—recognizing that having some negative impact is natural and justified? And how can we also have a larger positive impact—recognizing that we're not just created to be less of a curse; we're also created to be a blessing?

Obstacles in the Church

Much more can be and has been said about our biblical role and relationship with creation.[12] The point here is that creation care is an integral part of our discipleship and witness, and it runs all throughout Scripture.

Thankfully, this message is getting out more and more in our churches, especially across my millennial generation. When I'm out speaking about creation care, I often ask for a show of hands from those who have already heard a talk on this topic. Ten years ago, when I first started, few hands were raised. Today, however, it's not unusual for a quarter to half of the people in the audience to respond positively. That's progress worth celebrating.

At the same time, however, there's still much room for growth. What's behind this ongoing blind spot? What's still holding back far too many of our evangelical churches and communities from a more robust and faithful engagement in creation care? And, while more millennials seem to be aware and supportive of environmental action, why does there appear to be more entrenched reluctance or opposition from older generations?

There are numerous reasons (dare I say excuses?) given for why some Christians resist engaging more fully in creation care. There are eight obstacles that I come across most often.

1. *The world is going to burn anyway.* Certain interpretations of Scripture (2 Pet. 3:7 and 10 in particular) paint a picture of a world that will be destroyed by fire at the end. Therefore, the argument goes, it's a waste of time to care for creation when our focus should be on saving souls. Regardless of what one believes about the end times—and many, such as prominent New Testament scholar N. T. Wright, advocate a very different understanding, one where the world is restored—that is no license for living poorly on the earth now. God values his creation, it brings him glory, and he created us to care for it, no matter what is to come in the future. In the same way, we strive to care for our bodies now even though (spoiler alert) we will one day die and decompose. And what parents would look at their newborn baby with love and, realizing the child will grow up and one day die, decide she or he just isn't worth their care?[13] That would clearly be biblically unfaithful and criminally negligent.

2. *It's just not my thing.* Sometimes creation care is incorrectly viewed as a hobby or special interest for select people to get involved with as it fits their passion. But that's not what the Bible portrays. We are all created in the image of God for the purpose of ruling this world on his behalf. True, we're not all called to be full-time vocational/professional environmentalists. But we all do have an impact on creation by virtue of being alive—that's just natural and unavoidable—and we all also have a responsibility for doing our part to care. Given how diversely environmental issues intersect with so many other fields, many of us will find significant connections to creation care within whatever vocation we do feel called to.

3. *It's a good idea and that's good enough.* More and more Christians and churches are beginning to recognize and affirm that creation care truly is biblical. But it often stops there. Yet the Bible teaches that faith without works is dead (see James 2:26). And if we know what the right thing is to do, and we don't do it, then we are sinning (see James 4:17). Creation care isn't just an idea; it's a lifestyle that requires pursuing and involves transformation.

4. *People are more important.* Yes, people are important and, for that matter, creation care is almost always "people care" as well. At the same time, the rest of creation is important too. Creation isn't just valuable for the ways it's useful to us or enriches our lives with beauty; it's also intrinsically valuable for the sufficient reason that God says it is. Repeatedly throughout Genesis 1, God surveys creation at its various stages and declares it to be good—that's even before humans are introduced. And just as God blesses humans to be fruitful and fill the earth (see Gen. 1:28) he also earlier proclaims that same blessing over the birds and the fish (Gen. 1:22). People are important, but we're not the center of the universe. God is. And he values all of creation and calls us to do likewise.

5. *It's more expensive.* We're often okay with "going green" if it saves us money. And thankfully it often does. By being more energy efficient we save on energy bills, and the same is true with water. Sometimes we have to invest more money at the beginning—say, in more expensive energy-efficient light bulbs or appliances or buildings—but we end up making that money back over time. But there are also times when caring for creation will simply cost more. That can be limiting at times, but it doesn't mean we automatically forgo making a better choice because it's also more expensive. It means we have to carefully weigh the pros and cons and consider what the right course of action is in light of what God expects of us. As a mentor once reminded me, the gospel is not revenue neutral. We will often be called to do what's right even when it comes at a greater cost, whether financially or otherwise. And often, bad environmental decisions are also cheaper because they externalize some of the costs. Coal-generated electricity has been relatively cheap for so long because it doesn't take into account the cost of the tragic human and environmental damage that results from mining and burning coal. How can we more honestly view environmental goods and services, and creation as a whole, so that our stewardship decisions reflect true value and not just sticker prices?

6. *Climate change is too controversial.* Climate change is but one of many creation care issues facing us today, although it is an urgent and overriding concern. The problem is that much of the church has been so hesitant to engage on climate change for some time now that we're woefully out of touch and misinformed. There are few issues that get people worked up as quickly and heatedly as climate change. I recently spoke at a church where someone toward the back angrily interrupted the program and yelled over (and at) me until I actually had to end the talk. Science is not the problem—any informed person who knowingly chooses

to ignore more than 97 percent of the scientific community on such a consequential problem is taking an irresponsible risk with this planet.[14] I'm not okay dealing with the consequences of such inaction for the rest of my life (and for generations to come). Technology and policies are also not the problem—we have many good ideas that aren't getting implemented yet because we lack a level economic playing field with all sorts of perverse incentives and corrupt subsidies in place. We also lack the moral and political will to stand up to the fossil fuel industry and reform this entrenched but broken status quo in a timely manner. So it's time for us as the people of God to take a step back from the culture wars and political ideology to consider what we already know and how the changing climate is already impacting us. Christian relief and development experts are reporting that climate impacts have become a major threat around the world and are undoing much of the development progress that has been made over the last several decades. May God give us eyes to see justly and hearts to respond compassionately.

7. *There's no point acting until China and India do it first.* For many years the United States was the world's biggest polluter. Now China has eclipsed us (though per capita we are still far more polluting than China and will be for years to come). But why do we make a big deal of the speck of sawdust in our neighbor's eye and ignore the plank in our own? Jesus admonishes us: "You hypocrite, first take the plank out of your own eye, and then you will see clearly to remove the speck from your brother's eye" (Matt. 7:5). We simply can't afford to have the rest of the world develop in the same polluting ways we did. So we have to work together to find cleaner and healthier ways for development to proceed with earnest. Not doing the right thing because others aren't doing it yet, especially after we've had a decades-long head start doing things the dirty way, is a far cry from being Christlike.

8. *It's too political or partisan.* No matter what American politics currently suggests, the environment is not a liberal priority—or a conservative priority—it's a biblical mandate and a gospel calling within the lordship of Christ. As Christians, we have an opportunity to transcend the partisan polarization of our day and demonstrate what it can look like for people of every political persuasion to faithfully care for creation. If as Christians we can't find a way to transcend politics on an issue as biblical as this, then our ideology is greater than our theology; and we're in deep trouble.

Bearing God's Image

For far too long the American church has abdicated our responsibility or has merely paid lip service to creation care. Meanwhile, many others have stepped up to care for creation, even though not all of them acknowledge or follow the Creator. We owe them a debt of gratitude and respect, for they've been doing the work of the church while too many of God's people have been asleep at the wheel.

The cost of such unfaithfulness is heavy. It exerts a toll on our discipleship as well as our witness. It increases human suffering, and it deprives creation of those who should be its most faithful caretakers. And it goes against the revealed will of God in Scripture.

What will it take for creation care to truly become an integral part of our discipleship and witness across the whole faith? When will our churches stop paying lip service to the concept of caring for creation, and start living it out with conviction and commitment? How can we overcome the many excuses for not engaging more fully and become known instead as a people who are serious about the earth and the well-being of everything in it?

No matter what the obstacle, nothing need hold us back from renewing our biblical role as caretakers of God's world. Many of us millennials do not need convincing of the importance of creation care, but we do need more leadership from our leaders. We do need more help and support from our elders. And we do eagerly await the day when God's people from all generations and backgrounds awaken and come together as one body, testifying in word and deed that this is our Father's world and, behold, he makes all things new (see Rev. 21:5).

Response by Ron Sider

Ben is right that the environmental crisis (especially global warming) is enormously serious and that many Christians, especially evangelicals, are not engaged. And his question about what it would take to change that neglect is urgent. In response, I want to share a story that demonstrates that change is possible and then outline how I think a better theological foundation could undergird still more progress.

Sometime in 1990, I received a call from Paul Gorman in New York—a person I had never met or even heard of before. Paul told me he was organizing a gathering of religious leaders to respond to an appeal from the scientific community (including distinguished Nobel Laureates) on the environment, saying that they desperately needed the help of religious leaders if we were to avoid environmental disaster. Paul wanted me to help bring a few key evangelical leaders to the meeting.

I agreed and over the course of the next two years, the National Religious Partnership on the Environment (NRPE) emerged. The NRPE was and is an unusual coalition with four partners: the National Council of Churches, the US Conference of Catholic Bishops, the Coalition on the Environment and Jewish Life, and the Evangelical Environmental Network (EEN).

Since the EEN was based in my organization, Evangelicals for Social Action, I was deeply involved in its work and in the work of the larger partnership (NRPE). For a decade and more, it was painfully obvious that the evangelical community had made significantly less progress than Catholic, mainline Protestant, and Jewish communities in engagement on the environment. But EEN worked hard developing an evangelical theological statement for prominent evangelical leaders to sign and disseminating literature for congregational use. In 1995–96, EEN played a key role in protecting the Endangered Species Act. ("We won," a prominent secular environmentalist said, "because of the evangelicals.") And in 2002, EEN launched the highly visible campaign called "What Would Jesus Drive?"

Slowly an increasing number of evangelical leaders embraced a concern for creation care. In 2006, EEN launched a strong declaration on climate change, "The Evangelical Climate Initiative," and hundreds of prominent evangelical leaders signed it. After a little more than twenty years of vigorous work by EEN and others, it is clear that, even though we still have leagues to go, the evangelical world has made some significant progress in caring for God's creation. It takes hard, persistent work, but change is possible.

Solid biblical theology is also important if we want to develop and sustain a powerful Christian movement for creation care that can avoid devastating consequences from climate change and pass on a decent world to our grandchildren. Sometimes, radical theological ideas articulated (or *allegedly* espoused) by some environmentalists have discouraged some Christians from seriously embracing creation care.

In fact, however, the Bible offers a solid theological framework for thinking about the nonhuman creation and the relationship of human beings to it.[15] In fact, biblical faith provides the best foundation for being an environmentalist. God's revelation demands that we actively care for creation.

Five biblical principles are especially important. First, whereas a one-sided view of either God's transcendence or immanence compounds our problems, a biblical combination of both points the way through our dilemmas. If we focus only on God's immanence (his presence in the world), we end up in pantheism where everything is divine and good as it is. If we talk only about God's transcendence (his radical separateness from creation), we may end up seeing nature as a mere tool to be used at human whim.

The biblical God is both immanent and transcendent. He is not a cosmic watchmaker who wound up the global clock and now lets it run on its own. God continues to work in the creation. In Job we read that God gives orders to the morning (38:12), that the eagle soars at God's command (39:27), and that God provides food for the ravens when their young cry out in hunger (38:41). The Creator, however, is also radically distinct from the creation. Creation is finite, limited, dependent; the Creator is infinite, unlimited, and self-sufficient.

Second, we should gratefully learn all we can from the book of nature without in any way abandoning biblical revelation. Matthew Fox, a radical former Roman Catholic theologian (the Vatican has disciplined him), has urged that we turn from a theology centered on sin and redemption and develop a "creation spirituality." Nature is our primary revelation, Fox says. When Fox tells us that we can get most or all the revelation we need from creation, our firm response must be that the biblical revelation of redemption from sin through Jesus Christ is as true and essential as ever in our environmental age.

Third, human beings are both interdependent with the rest of creation and unique within it because we alone have been created in the divine image and given stewardship over the earth. Christians have at times forgotten our interdependence with the rest of creation. Our daily existence depends on water, sun, and air. Everything is interdependent in the global ecosystem. The emissions from our cars contribute to the destruction of trees—trees that convert the carbon dioxide we exhale into the oxygen we need to survive. Christians today must recover an appreciation of our dependence on the trees and flowers, the streams and forests. Unless we do, we shall surely perish.

But the Bible insists on two other things about humanity: human beings alone are created in the image of God, and we alone have been given a special "dominion" or stewardship. It is a biblical truth, not speciesism, to say that only human beings—and not trees and animals—are created in the image of God (Gen. 1:27). This truth is the foundation of our God-given mandate to have dominion over the nonhuman creation (Gen. 1:28; Ps. 8).

Tragically—and arrogantly—we have distorted dominion into domination. Lynn White, the historian who several decades ago wrote a famous essay blaming Christianity for environmental decay, was partly correct. But it is a misunderstanding of the Bible, not God's Word itself, that is at fault here.

Genesis 2:15 says the Lord put us in the garden "to work it and take care of it." The word 'abad, translated "work," means "to serve." The related noun actually means "slave" or "servant." The word shamar, translated "take care of," suggests watchful care and preservation of the earth. In fact, shamar is the word used five times in Psalm 121 to describe the wonderful way God constantly "watches over" us without ever sleeping:

I lift up my eyes to the mountains—
    where does my help come from?
My help comes from the LORD,
    the Maker of heaven and earth.
He will not let your foot slip—
    he who watches over you will not slumber;
indeed, he who watches over Israel
    will neither slumber nor sleep.
The LORD watches over you—
    the LORD is your shade at your right hand;
the sun will not harm you by day,
    nor the moon by night.
The LORD will keep you from all harm—
    he will watch over your life;
the LORD will watch over your coming and going
    both now and forevermore.

Psalm 121

What an awesome task we have to watch over the earth the way God watches over us! We are to serve and watch lovingly over God's good garden, not destroy it.

The Old Testament offers explicit commands designed to prevent exploitation of the earth. Every seventh year, for instance, the Israelites' land was to lie fallow because "the land is to have a year of sabbath rest" (Lev. 25:4). Failure to provide this sabbatical for the land was one reason for the Babylonian captivity (Lev. 26:34, 42–43). "I will remember the land," Yahweh declared (26:42).

God summons us to both watch over and care for the non-human creation and also recognize our unique status. If we have no different status from that of animals and plants, we cannot eat them for food or use them to build civilizations. Because we do have a special status, however, we do not need to apologize to brother carrot when we have lunch. We are free to use the resources of the earth for our own purposes. Created in the divine image, we alone have been placed in charge of the earth. At the same time, our dominion must be the gentle care of a loving gardener, not the callous exploitation of a self-centered lord. So we should not wipe out species or waste the nonhuman creation. Only a careful, stewardly use of plants and animals by human beings is legitimate.

Fourth, a God-centered, rather than a human-centered, worldview respects the independent worth of the nonhuman creation. Christians have too easily and too often fallen into the trap of supposing that the nonhuman creation has worth only as it serves human purposes. This, however, is not a biblical perspective.

Genesis 1 makes it clear that all creation is good—good, according to the story, even before our first ancestors arrived on the scene. Colossians 1:16 reveals that all things are created *for* Christ. And according to Job 39:1–2, God watches over the mountain goat and the doe, counting the months of pregnancy and watching over them when they give birth! The first purpose of the nonhuman creation, then, is to glorify God, not to serve us.

> The heavens declare the glory of God;
>   the skies proclaim the work of his hands.
> Day after day they pour forth speech;
>   night after night they reveal knowledge.
> They have no speech, they use no words;
>   no sound is heard from them.
> Yet their voice goes out into all the earth,
>   their words to the end of the world.
>
> Psalm 19:1–4

It is important to note that God has a covenant not only with persons but also with the nonhuman creation. After the flood, God made a covenant with the animals as well as with Noah: "I now establish my covenant with you and with your descendants after you and with every living creature that was with you—the birds, the livestock and all the wild animals, all those that came out of the ark with you—every living creature on earth" (Gen. 9:9–10).

Jesus recognized God's covenant with the whole of creation when he noted how God feeds the birds and clothes the lilies (Matt. 6:26–30). The nonhuman creation has its own worth and dignity apart from its service to humanity.

Insisting on the independent dignity of the nonhuman creation does not mean that we ignore the biblical teaching that it has been given to us for our stewardship and use. Always, however, our use of the nonhuman creation must be a thoughtful stewardship that honors creation's dignity and worth in the eyes of the Creator.

Finally, God's cosmic plan of redemption includes the nonhuman creation. This fact provides a crucial foundation for building a Christian theology for an environmental age. The biblical hope that the whole created order, including the material world of bodies, rivers, and trees, will be part of the final kingdom confirms that the created order is good and important.

The Bible's affirmation of the material world can be seen most clearly in Christ himself: not only did the Creator enter his creation by becoming flesh and blood to redeem us from our sin, but the God-man was resurrected *bodily* from the tomb. The goodness of the created order is also revealed in how the Bible describes the coming kingdom: the marriage supper of the Lamb, where we will feast on bread, wine, and all the glorious fruit of the earth. The material world is so good that we delight in the fruit of the earth, not just now but even in the coming kingdom!

Christians have sometimes ignored the significance of the body and the material world, focusing all their energy on preparing the soul for some future immaterial, invisible existence in a spiritual heaven. Interestingly, there are striking parallels between such Christians and Eastern monists who tell us that the material world is an illusion to be escaped so that we can discover the divine spark within and eventually merge with the All and lose all individual identity. Neither view would be of much help to environmentalists. If the material world is evil or an illusion, why worry about it?

Biblical faith, however, is radically different. Every part of the material world comes from the loving hand of the Creator who calls it into being out of nothing and declares it very good. Unlike the Creator, the creation is finite and limited, but it is not an illusion. Nor is it a result of blind, materialistic chance, although the Creator lovingly nurtured it into existence over the course of a long evolutionary history.

The prophets often spoke of the impact of human sin on nature (Gen. 3:17–18; Isa. 24:4–6; Hosea 4:1–3). But they also foresaw that in the messianic time nature would share in the wonderful fruit of salvation: "In that day I will make a covenant for them with the beasts of the field, the birds in the sky and the creatures that move along the ground" (Hosea 2:18; see Isa. 55:12–13; Hosea 2:16–23).

In biblical faith, the material world is so good that the Creator of the galaxies actually became flesh once in the time of Caesar Augustus. Indeed, the material world is so good that not only did Jesus devote much time to restoring broken bodies, he also arose bodily from death and promised to return to complete his victory over every form of brokenness in persons, nature, and civilization.

According to biblical faith, God's cosmic plan of restoration includes the whole creation, not just individual "souls." In Colossians 1:15–20, we read that God intends to reconcile all things, "whether things on earth or things in heaven," through Jesus Christ. That does not mean that everyone will be saved; rather, it means that Christ's restoration will finally extend to all of creation. The fall's corruption of every part of creation will be corrected.

Paul says that at the end of history as we now experience it, Christ will return not only to usher believers into a life of restored bodily existence in the presence of God but also to restore the whole nonhuman creation. "The creation itself will be liberated from its bondage to decay and brought into the freedom and glory of the children of God" (Rom. 8:21).[16]

Some people think 2 Peter 3:7–10 teaches something quite different—namely, the total destruction of the heavens and earth rather than their renewal. The Revised Standard Version, for example, translates verse 10: "the earth and the works that are upon it will be burned up." Some scholars, however, argue that the passage refers to purification by fire rather than total destruction.[17] And the New International Version translates it: "The earth and everything done in it will be laid bare"—presumably exposed so that God can punish all evil.

Just a few verses later, 2 Peter 3 says Christians await a "new heaven and new earth" (v. 13). It would be possible to understand the author to mean that this present world will be totally destroyed at the final judgment and that later God will create a totally new heaven and earth. But that would contradict Paul in Romans 8:21. Furthermore, Isaiah uses the language of the creation of a new heaven and earth ("See, I will create new heavens and a new earth. The former things will not be remembered" [Isa. 65:17]). But then the passage goes on to describe the historical city of Jerusalem, which has been purged of evil so that people live happily to old age, build houses, and plant vineyards (65:18–23). Obviously, the language of the creation of a new heaven and earth is powerful metaphorical language to refer to the restoration of justice and righteousness in Jerusalem. And indeed, Revelation 21–22 draws on precisely the same imagery from Isaiah 65 to depict the dramatic transformations at Christ's second coming when all evil will be removed and the Lord will dwell with his people on a transformed earth.

The last book of the Bible uses a beautiful metaphor about the tree of life growing beside an unpolluted river, pure as crystal, that purges human civilization of its brokenness and evil so that the glory and honor of the nations may enter into the holy city of the future (Rev. 21:22–22:2). Unlike Christian Platonists and Hindu monists who see the material world as evil or an illusion to escape, Christians believe that the material world matters so much that the Creator will eventually restore its broken beauty. Knowing God's grand design, Christians work to initiate now what God will later complete.

The Christian hope for Christ's return must be joined with our doctrine of creation. Knowing that we are summoned by the Creator to be wise gardeners caring for God's good earth, knowing the hope that someday the earth will be restored, Christians should be vigorous participants in creation care.

DISCUSSION QUESTIONS

1. In what ways do you personally care for God's creation? Why is this important to you?
2. What would be the next step for you to take in being a better caretaker of God's creation? Is there a book you'd like to read or a particular part of your life you'd like to change?

3. In what ways does your church care for God's creation? Does paper get purchased according to the price tag on the case or according to how many trees had to be cut down to make it? Is there a community garden? How many Styrofoam coffee cups are sent each week to the landfill to take up space for the next five hundred years? Who in your church thinks about the hundreds of questions like these?

4. How does your church teach creation care to people? Through sermons? Classes? The examples of church members?

5. According to Genesis 1:26–28, there is a purpose for which God created us. How could you influence your church to take that purpose more seriously?

Conclusion

Jesus at the Center

There are growing intergenerational tensions in the family of God over what it means to be faithful today, and we need to find better ways to work through these issues.

We come from different contexts and perspectives, and often struggle to understand or relate to one another. Overcoming this involves intentionally reaching out, opening up, and being vulnerable. It takes humility, patience, and sacrificial love. It may often be hard, and sometimes we'll get hurt. But it's still both possible and worthwhile. We all have weaknesses, prejudices, and blind spots, both as individuals and as generations. Often it's our differences that help draw these out into the light where we can deal with and grow from them.

Throughout this book, we have sought to explore a charitable and constructive dialogue around some of the major challenges facing the church today. We intentionally didn't focus on the more stereotypical frustrations our generations have toward one another—such as whether traditional or contemporary worship music is better—not because these aren't real differences to work through, but because they're not the most important ones.

We also recognize that generations are very diverse and include individuals of all persuasions on any given subject. So we will always struggle to be fully and fairly nuanced in these conversations and to truly listen to one another. Just because things are complex, however, doesn't mean we can't dialogue about them in meaningful ways. We hope that this book has helped to show that, underneath our differences, we have lots of common ground and significant room for growth.

This dialogue must continue. We may not always get along or see eye to eye, but we're stuck with one another, and for the better. We're family, not related by human blood or law—as strong as that is—but by the supremely powerful blood of Christ and covenant of God. The reality is that what separates us is far less significant than what binds us together. Or rather, *who* binds us together. As the apostle Paul writes in Colossians 1:15–20:

> [Christ] is the image of the invisible God, the firstborn over all creation. For in him all things were created: things in heaven and on earth, visible and invisible, whether thrones or powers or rulers or authorities; all things have been created through him and for him. He is before all things, and in him all things hold together. And he is the head of the body, the church; he is the beginning and the firstborn from among the dead, so that in everything he might have the supremacy. For God was pleased to have all his fullness dwell in him, and through him to reconcile to himself all things, whether things on earth or things in heaven, by making peace through his blood, shed on the cross.

Regardless of the question or problem, the key to moving forward faithfully—and moving forward together—is that Jesus, as revealed to us in the Bible, must be our center. And the more we are defined by Jesus and the Bible, the more we will also be able to relate to one another.

One common analogy is of a bicycle wheel, with each of us on a spoke and Jesus at the hub. The farther away we are on our respective spokes from the hub, the farther away we also are from one another. The closer we are to our center, however, the closer we come to one another. This reality doesn't ignore our diverse contexts or deny our individual perspectives. Rather, it fulfills them through the good news that Christ has destroyed all barriers and divisions by his work on the cross, and that he redeems and reconciles us as one new people before him. After all, this is Christ's church, not ours.

At the end of the day, we seek first the kingdom of God and trust that everything else, whether quibbles or questions or concerns or challenges, will be sorted out as well. We go out into God's good but groaning world as we are sent, to make disciples of all nations and all generations, trusting in Jesus's promise that he will be with us to the very end of the age. Generations come, and generations go. But Jesus Christ is the same yesterday and today and forever (Heb. 13:8).

So we say together, and with joy, "Now to him who is able to do immeasurably more than all we ask or imagine, according to his power that is at work within us, to him be glory in the church and in Christ Jesus throughout all generations for ever and ever! Amen" (Eph. 3:20–21).

Notes

Chapter 2: Will You Remember Evangelism?

1. See further chap. 6 ("Social Sin") in my *Rich Christians in an Age of Hunger*, 6th ed. (Nashville: Thomas Nelson, 2015).

2. Ronald J. Sider, "Evangelicals and Structural Injustice: Why Don't They Understand It and What Can Be Done?" in *First the Kingdom of God: Global Voices on Global Mission*, ed. Daniel K. Darko and Beth Snodderly (Pasadena, CA: William Carey International University Press, 2014), 257–63.

3. See chaps. 3 and 4 of my *Good News and Good Works: A Theology for the Whole Gospel* (Grand Rapids: Baker, 1999).

4. See the discussion in ibid., 163.

5. See ibid., chap. 10.

6. See ibid., chap. 9.

7. It is even true that the best of human civilization will somehow be purged of evil and taken up into the new Jerusalem (Rev. 21:24–22:2).

8. See chap. 4 in my *Cup of Water, Bread of Life* (Grand Rapids: Zondervan, 1994), 71–73.

9. See the superb book showing how Paul's high Christology began in his earliest writings: Gordon D. Fee, *Pauline Christology: An Exegetical-Theological Study* (Grand Rapids: Baker Academic, 2007), 49. See also Larry W. Hurtado, *How on Earth Did Jesus Become God? Historical Questions about Earliest Devotion to Jesus* (Grand Rapids: Eerdmans, 2005).

10. Acts 17:30–31; 2 Cor. 5:10–11; John 5:28–29; Matt. 16:27.

11. See my discussion in *Good News and Good Works*, 130–39—including that the New Testament does not exclude the possibility that persons may have an opportunity to embrace Christ after they die.

12. Pew Research Center's Religion and Public Life Project, "America's Changing Religious Landscape," May 12, 2015, http://religions.pewforum.org/reports.

13. Barna Group, "Is Evangelism Going Out of Style?" December 18, 2013, https://www.barna.org/barna-update/faith-spirituality/648-is-evangelism-goi#.

Chapter 3: Will You Reaffirm Truth as You Learn from Postmodernism?

1. For a critique of foundationalism, see Alvin Plantinga, *Warranted Christian Belief* (New York: Oxford University Press, 2000), 82–107. See also the careful articulation of a "critical-realist epistemology" by N. T. Wright, *The New Testament and the People of God* (Minneapolis: Fortress, 1992), 32–46.

2. Quoted in Merold Westphal, *Whose Community? Which Interpretation? Philosophical Hermeneutics for the Church* (Grand Rapids: Baker Academic, 2009), 60.

3. Alan Sokal, "Transgressing the Boundaries: Towards a Transformative Hermeneutics of Quantum Gravity," *Social Text* (Spring/Summer 1996): 217–52.

4. "A Physicist Experiments with Cultural Studies," *Lingua Franca* (May/June 1996): 62–64. For a long scholarly discussion of the whole incident, see John Guillory, "The Sokal Affair and the History of Criticism," *Critical Inquiry* 28, no. 2 (Winter 2002): 470–508.

5. As Merold Westphal rightly insists, that claim does not mean that for thinkers like Foucault, Derrida, and Gadamer "anything goes"—i.e., that any interpretation of a text is equally valid (Westphal, *Whose Community?*, 62). See, for example, the quotation from Derrida, which gives a significant role to traditional criticism (i.e., grammatical-historical exegesis). But see also the critique of Derrida in Nicholas Wolterstorff, *Divine Discourse: Philosophical Reflections on the Claim That God Speaks* (New York: Cambridge University Press, 1995), 153–70 (and also contra Ricoeur, 130–52).

6. Pope John Paul II, *The Splendor of Truth (Veritatis Splendor)* (Boston: St. Paul Books and Media, 1993), sec. 32.

7. John Paul places a much greater emphasis than I do on the natural law available to human reason as the way to discern morality. I emphasize much more the Bible as the place to discern God's revelation of moral truth. But I find the basic argument of the relationship between freedom and truth very helpful.

8. John Paul, *Splendor of Truth*, sec. 85, 87, emphasis in original.

9. See ibid., sec. 99.

10. Wolterstorff rightly emphasizes the importance of trying to discern what the author says (*Divine Discourse*, 130–70).

11. See Manfred T. Brauch, *Abusing the Scripture: The Consequences of Misreading the Bible* (Downers Grove, IL: IVP Academic, 2009), 225–49, esp. 229.

12. Great care, of course, must be exercised in using contemporary knowledge to understand what God intends to reveal to us in the Bible. What some people assert is assured scientific knowledge is really not that but dogmatic conclusions that result from their embrace of philosophical naturalism. See, for example, Carl Sagan, *The Demon-Haunted World: Science as a Candle in the Dark* (New York: Random House, 1995).

13. Christian Churches Together in the USA and the Global Christian Forum both represent very important recent instances where a much wider range of

Christians than ever before (Catholics, Orthodox Christians, evangelicals/Pente-costals, and mainline Protestants) have come to the same table to pray, worship, and talk together.

14. See Mark Noll's classic work *The Scandal of the Evangelical Mind* (Grand Rapids: Eerdmans, 1995), for more on this.

Chapter 4: Will You Keep Your Marriage Vows Better Than My Generation?

1. I do not mean to suggest that a life of singleness is less worthy or less Christian than a married life. Jesus and Paul were both single and indeed celebrated the advantages of celibate singleness.

2. Sylvia Ann Hewlett and Cornel West, *The War against Parents* (Boston: Houghton Mifflin, 1998), 35, emphasis in original.

3. For the bibliographic citations, see my *Just Generosity: A New Vision for Overcoming Poverty in America* (Grand Rapids: Baker Books, 2007), 161.

4. Ibid., 160.

5. Ibid., 161.

6. Ibid., 151–60.

7. David Popenoe, "The Controversial Truth: Two-Parent Families Are Better," letter, *New York Times*, December 26, 1992.

8. See New Testament scholar Craig Keener's careful argument that Jesus would have assumed that in the narrow situation where divorce was permissible, remarriage would also be permissible (Keener, *And Marries Another: Divorce and Remarriage in the Teaching of the New Testament* [Peabody, MA: Hendrickson, 1991]).

9. Bradley R. E. Wright, Christian Zozula, and W. Bradford Wilcox, "Bad News about the Good News: The Construction of the Christian-Failure Narrative," *Journal of Religion and Society* 14 (2012): 9.

10. Ibid. In my *Scandal of the Evangelical Conscience* (Grand Rapids: Baker Books, 2005), I relied heavily on data from the Barna Group. But Wright, Zozula, and Wilcox offer a significant critique of some of their methodology ("Bad News about the Good News," 11–12, 14–15).

11. W. Bradford Wilcox, "Conservative Protestants and the Family," in *A Public Faith: Evangelicals and Civic Engagement*, ed. Michael Cromartie (New York: Rowman & Littlefield, 2003), 63. See Wilcox's explanation in Andrew Walker, "No, Christianity Is Not Bad for Marriage," *Canon and Culture: Christianity and the Public Square* (website), February 11, 2104, www.canonandculture.com/no-christianity-is-not-bad-for-marriage-brad-wilcox-on-red-state-family-structure-and-conservative-protestantism/.

12. Wright, Zozula, and Wilcox, "Bad News about the Good News," 9. Numerous other studies show the same results (p. 10).

13. I also do not mean to suggest that one should continue to live with a physically abusive spouse. Separation for a time (one hopes with the strong, loving support of one's local congregation) is sometimes the right thing to do.

14. They provide excellent biblical and theological work. See especially Ronald W. Pierce, Rebecca Merrill Groothuis, and Gordon D. Fee, eds., *Discovering*

Biblical Equality: Complementarity without Hierarchy (Downers Grove, IL: InterVarsity, 2004); and the website of Christians for Biblical Equality (CBE) International, cbeinternational.org.

15. Les and Leslie Parrott, *Becoming Soul Mates: 52 Meditations to Bring Joy to Your Marriage* (Grand Rapids: Zondervan, 1995), 88.

16. In the following paragraphs, I have adapted a section from my *Living like Jesus* (Grand Rapids: Baker, 1999), 48–56.

17. The "divorce surge" across society appears to be getting better. *The New York Times* recently reported that the divorce rate peaked in the 1970s and 1980s and has been dropping ever since. Claire C. Miller, "The Divorce Surge Is Over but the Myth Lives On," *New York Times*, December 2, 2014, http://www.nytimes .com/2014/12/02/upshot/the-divorce-surge-is-over-but-the-myth-lives-on.html. Of course, there's a lot of nuance to these statistics: the divorce rate is still high among those who have not been to college, and more people are getting married later these days. Overall, however, the trend is positive. It's also encouraging to note that while some studies have suggested that the divorce rate among Christians is even greater than the societal average, these numbers drop off considerably when focused on those who attend church more regularly. Ed Stetzer, "Marriage, Divorce, and the Church: What Do the Stats Say, and Can Marriage Be Happy?," *The Exchange: A Blog by Ed Stetzer*, *Christianity Today*, February 14, 2014, http:// www.christianitytoday.com/edstetzer/2014/february/marriage-divorce-and-body -of-christ-what-do-stats-say-and-c.html. Active faith seems to have a strong positive influence on marriages, and that's good news. For more on Christian divorce rates, see sociologist Bradley Wright, "Statistics about Christian Divorce Rate," *Bradley Wright's Blog*, December 19, 2006, http://brewright.blogspot.com/2006 /12/christian-divorce-rates.html.

Chapter 5: Will You Lead the Church to a Better Stance on Homosexuality?

1. This chapter is longer than my other chapters, not because the topic is more important, but both because I have not written much previously on the topic and because the issue is a matter of intense debate.

2. See chap. 5, "Sins against the LGBTQ Community," in *Forgive Us: Confessions of a Compromised Faith*, by Mae Elise Cannon, Lisa Sharon Harper, Troy Jackson, and Soong-Chan Rah (Grand Rapids: Zondervan, 2014).

3. Richard Hays is right in saying that since the fall, all persons have a sinful nature that inclines us to all kinds of sinful acts. But I think it is confusing for Hays to deny that "a homosexual orientation is morally neutral because it is involuntary." *The Moral Vision of the New Testament* (San Francisco: Harper-SanFrancisco, 1996), 390.

As Christians who are only partly sanctified, we all experience temptations that arise, because of the fall, from our still partly twisted hearts—whether the inclination is to pride, materialism, or adulterous or homosexual acts. But there is a huge ethical distinction between feeling a temptation to a sinful action and acting on that temptation. Jesus's condemnation of lust as well as actual adultery

(Matt. 5:28) does not mean that a man's initial physical attraction to a woman who is not his wife is sin even though it happens because of the fall. One lusts in one's heart only when one dwells on the attraction and the possibility of acting upon it. The same is true of the attraction of a person with a gay orientation. Simply experiencing same-sex attraction and being aware of that but choosing not to act on that is no more sinful than experiencing an inclination to adultery, drunkenness, lying, or greed but choosing not to act on that.

4. I have written on this elsewhere—e.g., "Bearing Better Witness," *First Things*, December 2010, 47–50.

5. There are, of course, a number of texts that describe and condemn sexual intercourse outside of marriage.

6. James V. Brownson is probably correct that the phrase in Gen. 2:24 about the man and woman becoming "one flesh" refers first of all to the formation of a new social unit or "kinship group," i.e., a new family. And he is almost certainly correct in rejecting Robert Gagnon's argument that Gen. 1:27–28 and Gen. 2:20–25 speak of an initially undifferentiated human being (Gen. 1) that then gets divided in Gen. 2 into two halves (male and female) that therefore need to be reunited in sexual intercourse (Brownson, *Bible, Gender, Sexuality: Reframing the Church's Debate on Same-Sex Relationships* [Grand Rapids: Eerdmans, 2013], 26–37) and elsewhere. But that does not mean that Gen. 1 and 2 do not refer at all to sexual intercourse between man and woman. Nor does Brownson's discussion undermine the view that Gen. 1 and 2 suggest that the Creator's design for intercourse is that between a man and a woman.

7. Isa. 5:1–7; 54:5–7; 61:10; 62:4–5; Jer. 2:20–3:3; 31:32; Ezek. 16:32; Hosea 1–3; Matt. 22:1–14; 25:1–13; Mark 2:19–20; John 3:29; Eph. 5:30–32; Rev. 19:7–9; Robert A. J. Gagnon, *The Bible and Homosexual Practice: Texts and Hermeneutics* (Nashville: Abingdon, 2001), 439n156.

8. Brownson argues that the Bible does not exclude committed same-sex intercourse, but even he acknowledges that "whenever the Bible uses the language of 'one flesh,' it is referring, usually explicitly, to unions between a male and a female" (*Bible, Gender, Sexuality*, 104).

9. Gagnon, *Bible and Homosexual Practice*, 44–56.

10. Hays, *Moral Vision*, 381.

11. For a thoughtful advocacy of these and similar views (and citations of a great deal of the literature), see Brownson, *Bible, Gender, Sexuality*. For a critique of these views, see Hays, *Moral Vision*, 388–99; Stanley J. Grenz, *Welcoming but Not Affirming* (Louisville: Westminster John Knox, 1998), 81–130; Gagnon, *Bible and Homosexual Practice*, 254–302, 341–486, and elsewhere.

12. For refutation of the idea that Rom. 1:26 condemns male-female intercourse during a woman's menstruation rather than female-female sex, see Bernadette J. Brooten, *Love between Women: Early Christian Responses to Female Eroticism* (Chicago: University of Chicago Press, 1996), 247–53.

13. David Gushee suggests that "because arguments from God's purported design in creation have proven remarkably problematic in Christian history, do not rely on them for sexual ethics" (*Changing Our Mind* [Canton, MI: Read the

Spirit Books, 2014], 94). But Jesus did precisely that. His teaching on divorce returns explicitly to God's design in creation (Matt. 19:3–6).

14. Gagnon, *Bible and Homosexual Practice*, 290.

15. We cannot know whether or not part of Paul's argument is a reference to the obvious physical anatomical fit of male and female sexual organs. But I have never understood why this obvious anatomical fit is not one valid argument in favor of the traditional understanding of the proper place for sexual intercourse.

16. Hays, *Moral Vision*, 387. Brownson has a long discussion on the meaning of "nature" in his text (*Bible, Gender, Sexuality*, 223–55), but nothing in his argument excludes the possibility that an important part of Paul's argument is that same-sex acts are contrary to what God wills for the created order.

17. Brooten says that Paul was probably thinking of Leviticus (*Love between Women*, 284).

18. Hays, *Moral Vision*, 382. See also Gagnon, *Bible and Homosexual Practice*, 306–12, for a discussion of various interpretations of the word.

19. For numerous citations, see Gagnon, *Bible and Homosexual Practice*, 316–32.

20. Robin Scroggs, *The New Testament and Homosexuality* (Philadelphia: Fortress, 1983), 83, 106–8.

21. Hays, *Moral Vision*, 382.

22. Ibid.

23. Dan O. Via and Robert A. J. Gagnon, *Homosexuality and the Bible: Two Views* (Minneapolis: Fortress, 2003), 93.

24. John J. McNeill, *Church and the Homosexual*, 3rd ed. (Boston: Beacon Press, 1988), 59–60.

25. Quoted in Grenz, *Welcoming but Not Affirming*, 87.

26. E.g., Scroggs, *New Testament and Homosexuality*, 123–29; Victor P. Furnish, *The Moral Teaching of Paul: Selected Issues*, rev. ed. (Nashville: Abingdon, 1985), 52–82; Martti Nissinen, *Homoeroticism in the Biblical World: A Historical Perspective* (Minneapolis: Fortress, 1998), 124–25 and elsewhere.

27. Brownson, *Bible, Gender, Sexuality*, 155–56 and elsewhere.

28. Furnish, *Moral Teaching of Paul*, 60–65. See other examples in Gagnon, *Bible and Homosexual Practice*, 380–81n47. There were some ancient moralists who thought this way and condemned this activity.

29. Hays, *Moral Vision*, 388. Brooten (*Love between Women*, 242–45) agrees with Hays that Paul means to condemn all same-sex intercourse.

30. Brownson, *Bible, Gender, Sexuality*, 155. See also 156. Brownson does briefly refer to Plato's *Symposium* (229–30) but then argues that since there is no evidence of Jews and Christians of Paul's time speaking of a same-sex orientation, we can assume that Paul knew nothing of the idea of a homosexual orientation.

31. Plato, *Symposium* 181B–D; quoted in Gagnon, *Bible and Homosexual Practice*, 351–52.

32. Plato, *Symposium* 191E–192C, 192E, 193C, emphasis added; quoted in Gagnon, *Bible and Homosexual Practice*, 354–55; see also 356–58.

33. Brooten, *Love between Women*, 3. In this book, Brooten provides considerable evidence from antiquity for persons viewed as having "a long-term or

even life-long homoerotic orientation" (9). For the evidence from astrologers, see 115–41.

34. Ibid., 143ff. For additional ancient sources that knew of a lifelong homoerotic identity, see also Robert Gagnon, "Does the Bible Regard Same-Sex Intercourse Intrinsically Sinful?" in *Christian Sexuality: Normative and Pastoral Principles*, ed. Russell E. Saltzman (Minneapolis: Kirk House, 2003), 141–46.

35. See Brooten, *Love between Women*, 275–80, 302; and Nissinen, *Homoeroticism in the Biblical World*, 105, 107, 129, etc.

36. Some people argue this view, but the scientific data do not support this argument. See the detailed discussion of the literature in Mary Stewart Van Leeuwen, "Neurohormonal Wars: Old Questions and Dubious Debates in the Psychology of Gender," *Books and Culture*, September/October 2012, 11–15; and part 2, November/December 2012, 11–15. The best current scientific research rejects a one-sided biological determinism. Both genetic and cultural factors are significant in shaping our sexual identity.

37. See my *Good News and Good Works* (Grand Rapids: Baker, 1999), 65–66, for more examples.

38. For careful analysis of all texts and issues, see Ronald W. Pierce, Rebecca Merrill Groothuis, and Gordon D. Fee, eds., *Discovering Biblical Equality: Complementarity without Hierarchy* (Downers Grove, IL: InterVarsity, 2004).

39. See, further, William J. Webb, *Slaves, Women and Homosexuals: Exploring the Hermeneutics of Cultural Analysis* (Downers Grove, IL: InterVarsity, 2001); and Webb's two chapters in Pierce et al., *Discovering Biblical Equality*, 382–413.

40. Via and Gagnon, *Homosexuality and the Bible*, 95.

41. Ibid., 35.

42. Ibid., 96.

43. See Jenell Williams Paris, *The End of Sexual Identity: Why Sex Is Too Important to Define Who We Are* (Downers Grove, IL: InterVarsity, 2011).

44. Brownson, *Bible, Gender, Sexuality*, 142–43.

45. Wesley Hill, *Washed and Waiting: Reflections on Christian Faithfulness and Homosexuality* (Grand Rapids: Zondervan, 2010); Hill, *Spiritual Friendship: Finding Love in the Church as a Celibate Gay Christian* (Grand Rapids: Brazos, 2015); Eve Tushnet, *Gay and Catholic: Accepting My Sexuality, Finding Community, Living My Faith* (Notre Dame: Ave Maria Press, 2014).

46. Hays, *Moral Vision*, 390.

47. Brownson, *Bible, Gender, Sexuality*, 175. See also 170–77.

48. Gushee, *Changing Our Mind*.

49. John Boswell, *Christianity, Social Tolerance, and Homosexuality* (Chicago: University of Chicago Press, 1980).

50. See the careful review with a great deal of citations of relevant literature in Grenz, *Welcoming but Not Affirming*, 63–80.

51. Ibid., 80. Gushee, who argues for accepting covenantal gay sexual practice, agrees that "until very recently the Christian church in all of its major branches included as part of its 2000-year-old sexual morality a rejection of the moral legitimacy of sexual acts of persons of the same sex" (*Changing Our Mind*, 9).

52. *Catechism of the Catholic Church* (New York: Doubleday, 1995), 625; section 2357.

53. Ibid., 625–26; sections 2358, 2359.

54. Stanley S. Harakas, "The Stand of the Orthodox Church on Controversial Issues," Greek Orthodox Archdiocese of America (website), http://www.goarch.org/ourfaith/controversialissues.

55. The World Evangelical Alliance represents about 600 million Christians worldwide.

56. Protestants, for example, do not agree with the Catholic view that contraceptives are wrong because the chief end of marriage is procreation. See the discussion in Brownson, *Bible, Gender, Sexuality*, 110ff.

57. For example, a 2013 poll by the Barna Group found that 37 percent of "practicing Catholics" in the United States approved of same-sex sexual relationships. But only 15 percent of "practicing Protestants" approved—and that figure had moved very little from 13 percent ten years earlier (Barna Group, "America's Change of Mind on Same-Sex Marriage and LGBTQ Rights," Barna Group [website], July 3, 2013, https://www.barna.org/barna-update/culture/618-america-s-change-of-mind-on-same-sex-marriage-and-lgbtq-rights#.VEaiFa5wSJa).

58. In *Changing Our Mind*, Gushee unfortunately does not give any serious consideration to the option I embrace here, dismissing it quickly as "5b" of the "exclusionist" option.

59. See Tish Harrison Warren, "The Wrong Kind of Christian," *Christianity Today*, September 2014, 54–58.

60. In this chapter, I have not discussed the public policy aspects of this topic. For a careful discussion of the coming legal challenges, see a book written by lawyers (some of them for same-sex marriage): Douglas Laycock, Anthony R. Picarello, and Robin Fretwell Wilson, eds., *Same-Sex Marriage and Religious Liberty: Emerging Conflicts* (New York: Rowman & Littlefield, 2008). See also Stephen Monsma, *Pluralism and Freedom: Faith-Based Organizations in a Democratic Society* (New York: Rowman & Littlefield, 2013); and the materials of the organization Institutional Religious Freedom Alliance, www.irfalliance.org.

61. However, the slogan, "hate the sin, love the sinner" is not helpful. Emphasizing hate is dangerous. It is better to grieve over sin. In addition, the slogan too easily nurtures a "sinful them" and "good us" dichotomy. Temptation stalks us all. Galatians 6:1–3 recommends the right combination of gentleness and ethical clarity.

62. Though often lumped in with same-sex attraction, gender dysphoria is a somewhat distinct and equally important issue to consider. While the question of gender identity and dysphoria lies beyond the scope of this chapter, a book I've found helpful here is Mark Yarhouse's *Understanding Gender Dysphoria: Navigating Transgender Issues in a Changing Culture* (Downers Grove, IL: InterVarsity, 2015).

63. A. W. Tozer, *The Pursuit of God* (Amazon Digital Services, 2011), 20.

Chapter 6: Will We Live More Like Jesus?

1. D. Joseph and T. McKeehan, "What If I Stumble?" Recorded by DC Talk, *Jesus Freak* (Forefront/Virgin Records, 1995).

2. Rev. Peter Harris, speech about creation care, Wheaton College Chapel, Wheaton, IL, March 9, 2008.

3. Dietrich Bonhoeffer, *The Cost of Discipleship* (New York: Touchstone, 1995), 44–45.

4. Ibid., 45.

5. Ron Sider, *The Scandal of the Evangelical Conscience: Why Are Christians Living Just like the Rest of the World?* (Grand Rapids: Baker Books, 2005).

6. For a much longer discussion, see my *Good News and Good Works: A Theology for the Whole Gospel* (Grand Rapids: Baker, 1999), chaps. 3 and 4.

7. See ibid., chap. 5.

8. See my *Rich Christians in an Age of Hunger*, 6th ed. (Nashville: Thomas Nelson, 2015), chap. 6.

9. Ron Sider, *For They Shall Be Fed* (Dallas: Word, 1997).

10. See Sider, *Rich Christians*, chap. 3.

11. See my *Just Politics: A Guide for Christian Engagement*, 2nd ed. (Grand Rapids: Brazos, 2012), chap. 5.

12. Stanley Hauerwas and William H. Willimon, *Resident Aliens: Life in the Christian Colony* (Nashville: Abingdon, 1990). The book has been reprinted several times.

Chapter 7: Will We Renew Our Political Witness?

1. "Congress Less Popular than Cockroaches, Traffic Jams," Public Policy Polling, January 8, 2013, http://www.publicpolicypolling.com/pdf/2011/PPP_Release_Natl_010813_.pdf.

2. John Stott, "John Stott: Four Ways Christians Can Influence the World," *Christianity Today* 55, no. 10 (2011): 38.

3. Ben Lowe, *Doing Good Without Giving Up: Sustaining Social Action in a World That's Hard to Change* (Downers Grove, IL: InterVarsity, 2014).

4. Mahatma Gandhi, *Autobiography: The Story of My Experiments with Truth*, trans. Mahadev Desai (Auckland, New Zealand: The Floating Press, 2009), 809.

5. Michael Gerson and Peter Wehner, *City of Man: Religion and Politics in a New Era* (Chicago: Moody Publishers, 2011), 135.

6. Ibid., 59.

7. Martin Luther King Jr., *Where Do We Go from Here: Chaos or Community?* (Boston: Beacon Press, 1967), 62.

8. See my *Fixing the Moral Deficit* (Downers Grove, IL: InterVarsity, 2012), 66–67.

9. See Christian Smith, *American Evangelicalism: Embattled and Thriving* (Chicago: University of Chicago Press, 1998), 187–93; and Michael O. Emerson and Christian Smith, *Divided by Faith* (New York: Oxford University Press, 2000), 94–96 and elsewhere.

10. See my "Evangelicals and Structural Injustice: Why They Don't Understand It and What Can Be Done?," in *First the Kingdom of God: Global Voices on Global Mission*, ed. Daniel K. Darko and Beth Snodderly (Pasadena, CA: William Carey International University Press, 2014), 257–63.

11. See my *Rich Christians in an Age of Hunger*, 6th ed. (Nashville: Thomas Nelson, 2015), chap. 6.

12. See Ronald J. Sider and Diane Knippers, eds., *Toward an Evangelical Public Policy: Political Strategies for the Health of the Nation* (Grand Rapids: Baker Books, 2005), 366.

13. See Brantley W. Gasaway, *Progressive Evangelicals and the Pursuit of Justice* (Chapel Hill: University of North Carolina Press, 2014); and David R. Swartz, *Moral Minority: The Evangelical Left in an Age of Conservatism* (Philadelphia: University of Pennsylvania Press, 2012).

14. See my *Completely Pro-Life: Building a Consistent Stance on Abortion, the Family, Nuclear Weapons, the Poor* (Downers Grove, IL: InterVarsity, 1987) and the extensive discussion of Gasaway and Swartz (see previous note).

15. "For the Health of the Nation," reprinted in Sider and Knippers, *Toward an Evangelical Public Policy*, 366, emphasis added.

16. David P. Gushee, *The Future of Faith in American Politics: The Public Witness of the Evangelical Center* (Waco, TX: Baylor University Press, 2008), esp. 87–120.

17. I do not mean to argue that large, temporary budget deficits are always wrong. Large budget deficits following the economic crash of 2007–2008 were necessary to avoid another great depression. But we cannot continue indefinitely with ongoing budget deficits. See my *Fixing the Moral Deficit*.

18. Ronald J. Sider, "Resigning from the AARP," *Huffington Post*, February 12, 2013, www.huffingtonpost.com/ronald-j-sider/aarp-lobby-social-security-medi care_b_2671577.html.

Chapter 8: Will We Reconcile Our Divisions Better?

1. Thanks to Warren Wong at Wheaton Chinese Alliance Church who pointed this out to me.

2. "Fast Facts about American Religion," Hartford Institute for Religion Research, http://hirr.hartsem.edu/research/fastfacts/fast_facts.html#denom.

3. Christena Cleveland, *Disunity in Christ: Uncovering the Hidden Forces That Keep Us Apart* (Downers Grove, IL: InterVarsity, 2013).

4. C. W. Perdue, J. F. Dovidio, M. B. Gurtman, and R. B. Tyler, "'Us' and 'Them': Social Categorization and the Process of Intergroup Bias," *Journal of Personality and Social Psychology* 59, no. 3 (September 1990): 475–86.

5. Wesley Granberg-Michaelson, *Unexpected Destinations: An Evangelical Pilgrimage to World Christianity* (Grand Rapids: Eerdmans, 2011).

6. See, for example, the 1999 "Joint Declaration on the Doctrine of Justification" issued by the Lutheran World Federation and the Catholic Church; the Lima Document from the World Council of Churches on Baptism, Eucharist and Ministry (1982); and the several statements by Evangelicals and Catholics Together.

7. That is not to affirm sexual promiscuity of any kind. See David Gushee's demand that all Christians, heterosexual and gay, who choose a sexual partner, reserve sexual intercourse to one married partner to which one is covenanted together for life. *Changing Our Mind* (Canton, MI: Read the Spirit Books, 2014), 100–106.

8. Dean M. Kelly, *Why Conservative Churches Are Growing* (New York: Harper & Row, 1972).

9. See my article on church discipline: "Watching over One Another in Love," *The Other Side*, May–June 1975, 13–15.

Chapter 9: Will We Recover Our Responsibility for God's Creation?

1. Source unknown. Sometimes called a Native American proverb, but there are many other attributions as well.

2. "7 Million Premature Deaths Annually Linked to Air Pollution," World Health Organization (website), March 25, 2014, http://www.who.int/mediacentre /news/releases/2014/air-pollution/en/.

3. "Global WASH Fast Facts," Centers for Disease Control and Prevention (website), November 8, 2013, http://www.cdc.gov/healthywater/global/wash_sta tistics.html.

4. "Hunger Statistics," World Food Programme (website), http://www.wfp .org/hunger/stats.

5. "Desertification," United Nations (website), http://www.un.org/en/events /desertificationday/background.shtml.

6. "Why Is Biodiversity in Crisis?" International Union for Conservation of Nature (website), October 14, 2010, https://www.iucn.org/iyb/about/biodiversity _crisis/.

7. Bryan Bender, "Chief of US Pacific Forces Calls Climate Biggest Worry," *Boston Globe*, March 9, 2013, http://www.bostonglobe.com/news/nation/2013/03/09 /admiral-samuel-locklear-commander-pacific-forces-warns-that-climate-change -top-threat/BHdPVCLrWEMxRe9IXJZcHL/story.html.

8. "Ocean Acidification: Facts and Figures," International Union for Conservation of Nature (website), December 17, 2012, http://www.iucn.org/media/facts _and_figures/?11675/Ocean-acidification—Facts-and-figures.

9. Portions of this section are adapted from an earlier blog post: Ben Lowe, "Good Friday Exposes Our Sinful Relationship with Creation," *Recovering Evangelical* (blog), April 22, 2011, http://recoveringevangelical.com/2011/04/good friday-2/.

10. Ken Wilson, *Jesus Brand Spirituality* (Nashville: Thomas Nelson, 2008), 59.

11. *The Cape Town Commitment*, part 1, sec. 7A, Lausanne Movement (website), http://www.lausanne.org/en/documents/ctcommitment.html#p1–7.

12. I've attempted to explore and unpack some of this in an earlier book titled *Green Revolution: Coming Together to Care for Creation* (Downers Grove, IL: InterVarsity, 2009); and others have published excellent resources, such as Steven Bouma-Prediger, *For the Beauty of the Earth: A Christian Vision for Creation Care* (Grand Rapids: Baker Academic, 2010); Edward R. Brown, *Our Father's World: Mobilizing the Church to Care for Creation* (Downers Grove, IL: InterVarsity, 2008); and Fred Van Dyke, *Between Heaven and Earth: Christian Perspectives on Environmental Protection* (Santa Barbara, CA: Praeger, 2010), to name just a few.

13. I first heard this example from Eric Norregaard in a talk he gave to the youth group at my church.

14. J. Cook et al, "Quantifying the Consensus on Anthropogenic Global Warming in the Scientific Literature," *Environmental Research Letters* 8 (June 2013), doi:10.1088/1748-9326/8/2/024024.

15. The next section is taken from my *Just Politics: A Guide for Christian Engagement* (Grand Rapids: Brazos, 2012), 172–76.

16. See N. T. Wright, *Surprised by Hope: Rethinking Heaven, the Resurrection, and the Mission of the Church* (New York: HarperOne, 2008).

17. See Al Wolters, "Worldview and Textual Criticism in 2 Peter 3:10," *Westminster Theological Journal* 49 (1987): 405–13. But see the critique of Wolters in Ryan Pelaza, "Echoes of Sodom and Gomorrah on the Day of the Lord: Intertextuality and Tradition in 2 Peter 3:7–13," a paper given at "Emerging Scholarship on the New Testament," Institute for Biblical Research's annual meeting, November 16–18, 2012, Chicago, 20.